Faith & Frenzy
Short Stories from
Kashmir

K L Chowdhury

Vitasta
Let Knowledge Spread

Published by
Renu Kaul Verma for
Vitasta Publishing Pvt. Ltd.
2/15, Ansari Road, Daryaganj,
New Delhi - 110 002
info@vitastapublishing.com

ISBN 978-93-80828-79-4

Layout and Cover by Vitasta Publishing Pvt. Ltd.
Print: Repro India Limited, Mumbai

These stories are mostly about the ordinary people of Kashmir, their relationships and bonds, their toils and tussles, their follies and foibles, their hopes and fears.
To them I dedicate this work.

Acknowledgements

I am grateful to my wife, Leela, and my siblings, Surinder and Robinder, for their encouragement and advice

Contents

1
THE POPLAR OF DISCORD

The poplar is ubiquitous in Kashmir. It grows with utmost ease almost anywhere in the valley—flat lands, plateaus and foothills. It lines boulevards, roads and avenues, and keeps company with the willow along riverbanks and around water bodies. It borders fields, backyards and gardens, and unlike the expansive walnut, it takes little space, just enough to stand upon, from where it grows straight up, tall and proud, almost speaking to the stars.

I had never heard of a dispute over a poplar till it happened right across in our neighbour's household. Unlike a walnut tree, the poplar is not something to which you grow terribly attached. A walnut tree has a big footprint and takes central place in any yard, grows slowly over decades after a lot of nurturing, and yields a coveted crop each year. It becomes a part of the family, another fond member. There is no such sentiment attached to the poplar which grows at the periphery, almost on its own, with little attention and effort. When properties are divided among heirs walnut trees are known to get in the way of division of land on which they stand. My father, an advocate, often regaled us with stories of litigation—even blood feuds—over walnut trees, and how his clients strained every nerve and spent every farthing to establish their claim on a coveted walnut tree. The dispute over a poplar was the first of its kind in his experience.

Devinder Nath Dhar, a retired widower, had moved from Srinagar downtown into our neighbourhood a few years before we did. Our northeastern side was demarcated from his plot partly by an outhouse that he owned and partly by a common wall. His main house stood in the middle of the yard. He had three sons, all married and with children. The eldest son, Pran Nath, lived with him. The second, Girdhari Lal, had settled in Bombay, and the youngest, Maharaj Krishan, had moved overseas and made England his home.

This was an inconspicuous household. Pran Nath Dhar had a wife who kept mostly to herself, and two children—a chubby boy and a pretty girl—who rarely mixed with the neighbourhood kids. Our house overlooked their garden. We hardly ever saw the family lounging around or socializing. At best, the couple sat together in the evenings at the bay window that faced our house directly, rarely looking across. Their children seldom played in the garden and the only time I saw them was when they came out of the house to go to school or go shopping.

Devinder Nath, the patriarch, was a little more sociable. He would visit us sometimes, wish us from across the window when we crossed each other's visual fields, and exchange pleasantries if we met on the street. He was worldly-wise and had carried out the duties expected of a middle class householder. He had educated his sons, who had now settled down in sound careers, married them into respectable families, bought the uptown property at the right time, renovated it and rented out the outhouse. He also planted poplars all along the periphery of his house. But he never made a will. When he died, the non-resident sons, Girdhari Lal and Maharaj Krishan, flew to Srinagar to attend the funeral. It was the first time we saw the three siblings together. They presented a picture of bonhomie and respectful indulgence, and gave their father a decent funeral, observing all the religious rites in the best tradition. At the end of the customary two-week mourning period, the visitors returned home while Pran Nath and his family resumed their lives in the house and withdrew into their customary solitude, seemingly content with their lot.

Surprisingly, Girdhari Lal's visits to Srinagar became more frequent after his father's demise. We knew about his arrival from the voices that emanated from the otherwise melancholy house, arguments that sometimes broke into sudden squeals. We did not intend to meddle in their affairs, until the day he came to seek my father's advice as a neighbour and a lawyer. It was the usual story of a property dispute threatening to degenerate into a feud between the brothers.

Girdhari Lal put forth his case: "Sir, you quite well know, this property was purchased by our revered father and stands in his name. I have been in Bombay for years now and have hardly ever lived in this house. It is Pran Nath who has been enjoying the use of this house all along. He lives in the big house and pockets the rent that accrues from the outhouse. While father was alive, I did not concern myself with the arrangements that might have existed between him and my brother. Now that he is no more, I have come here to press the claim for my share of the property. But he evades any serious discussion on the subject. He maintains that I am free to return and settle in the house, and that he owes me nothing of the rent since he looks after the property."

"Did you ask for a division of the property?" father asked.

"Yes, that is what I desire, a proper division or a sale. But he has been prevaricating; says it is too soon after the demise of father to discuss these things, and that he is not ready to sell the property, certainly not until both his children come of age."

"What did you say to that?"

"It may amount to waiting a decade or more, depending upon what he means by that statement." Girdhari Lal sighed in frustration and bared his suspicious mind, "I do not trust him. I feel he wants to cheat me of my share. Since I live far away, he might even dispose off the property without my knowledge."

"If he is not inclined to sell the property, he should have no objection to a division. Since he asks you to come and live here, let him give you your share. Then you will be at liberty to do with it what you like—live there or sell it off. What about your brother Maharaj Krishan? Have you sounded him out on this? Just because he has migrated to a foreign land does not strip him off his property rights," father reminded him.

"I am sorry, I have not. He has not written or phoned after his return to London. I will write to him right away," he replied apologetically.

"You should have discussed this with him while he was here during the funeral. You can not effect a division or sale of the property without his knowledge and consent."

"I agree. In fact, I am not worried about Maharaj Krishan; I am sure he will have no objection. It is Pran Nath who has to give up his intransigence."

Father probed him further. "Did you tell Pran Nath that you were coming to see me?"

"Yes sir, I suggested that we seek your counsel, but he does not approve of taking, what he thinks is a family problem, outside the family. Therefore I came here on my own after having failed to convince him. I do not believe we can sort this out without help, and I cannot think of a better person than you," he said with conviction.

"You do not live here, your brother does. He is my neighbour and it behives me not to take sides or offer advice unless all of you want my arbitration," father closed the argument.

On the face of it, this was a typical property dispute. But like the common cold that affects its victims differently, this property dispute had its own distinctiveness. Pran Nath was not interested in changing the status quo, and certainly not in selling off the property, so it seemed. Girdhari Lal was desperate to acquire his share. Mahraj Krsihan had not been sounded about the proposal to divide or dispose off the property. Assuming that they agreed in principle to a division rather than a sale, it would not be easy to divide the property into three equal shares the way it was laid out. The main house stood in the middle of the land and was designed for a single family. It would have to be shared by two brothers while the third would take the outhouse. Even then, it would not be easy to settle which one of the brothers was to get which share. In any case, father did not want to intervene unless all the brothers agreed to make him the arbiter.

Girdhari Lal returned to Bombay a few days later. Before he left, he informed father that Pran Nath had agreed to offer the rent collected on the outhouse to him. They would both write to their younger brother and wait for his response before taking the next step. It appeared that good sense had prevailed and the first step towards the resolution of the property dispute had been taken.

Life resumed its course in the Dhar house, calm from outside but an unseen ferment growing within. Pran Nath never sought my father's advice, never even referred to the dispute with his brother. We often saw him sitting alone at his window, lost in deep contemplation for hours on end.

Several weeks later, Girdhari Lal returned. We knew of it from the sudden rumblings of disquiet and discontent that rent the calm of the neighborhood, the two brothers arguing, shouting and swearing. The neighbours kept assiduously out of it, amusedly watching the developments from the sidelines, as the brothers fought it out behind the brick walls of the house.

Girdhari Lal came to see father again and whined about his brother's uncompromising attitude.

"I am sorry to bother you again, but I want to apprise you of the latest developments. There is good news; Maharaj Krishan has written that he is not interested in his share of the property. But, rather than making things easy, it has complicated the issue. Pran Nath is offering me the outhouse and the contiguous chunk of land, keeping the main house and a larger share of land to himself."

"That sounds unfair," father said sympathetically.

"He is no doubt offering suitable cash compensation for the shortfall in the land and the house," he explained.

"In that case it is not a bad deal. I see no problem," father responded.

"But I am in a hurry for the final settlement. I am not interested in holding on to any property in Kashmir since I have moved out permanently. I feel the only reasonable way out is for my brother to pay me for the half share at the prevailing market price or to sell the whole property and share the proceeds." He seemed adamant.

"Let us be reasonable. This place is centrally located. You cannot force your brother to sell the house in which his family is well settled and comfortable. Obviously, he wants to avoid any disruption that would result if he sold it now, when his children are attending school that is at walking distance from here. He has made you a good offer. If I were you, I would accept the outhouse and the land with it, and the cash compensation. You can sell it soon after if you want to," father gave his candid opinion.

"But Pran Nath says he does not have enough money to compensate me right away."

Father was a great believer in out-of-court settlements. "Why can't you agree to take part of the payment now and the balance in installments?" he suggested.

"I would, but I know how insincere my brother is. I am certain he has all the money he needs to settle this. He is an engineer of long standing and everyone knows of the fortunes engineers make in Kashmir. I have no patience with him; I want to sort this whole thing out now so I don't have to come here again." It seemed he had made up his mind.

"Why are you in such desperate hurry? After all, he is your own flesh and blood." Father was getting impatient with his obduracy.

"Because, I have little time and I do not want this issue hanging on for long. I am not in the best of health and there are many other personal and domestic issues to be sorted out. It will not be easy for me to come from Bombay frequently to find a buyer for my part of the property or to collect the installments from my brother. My kids are even younger than his and I hate to leave them with a legacy of disputes, litigation and family feuds. No, sir! I have come for the final resolution." He looked quite distraught and desperate and could neither hide the contempt for his brother nor the self-pity.

Father felt sad seeing the wretchedness writ large on his face. "Did you not explain your problems to your brother?" he asked.

"I did, but does he care? He might as well wish me dead before he parts with my share of the property." Girdhari Lal seemed adamantly opposed to his brother.

"Are you not judging him rather harshly? Relationships are much more important than properties."

"I have nothing against my brother; I am seeking a reasonable, amicable settlement," he insisted.

"There is another way out. You could give a power of attorney to a trusted person who can look after your interests here," father suggested.

"If I can't trust my own brother, how can I find a reliable person to whom I would give the power of attorney?" He was impervious to any suggestion.

Father gently dismissed him since he did not know what his role was as long as the brothers did not see eye to eye with each other nor sought his mediation. "Your noble father must be turning in heaven to see you brothers locked in this rivalry. I feel sorry for both of you and hope good sense prevails."

A couple of mornings later, we were witness to a bizarre

occurrence. There was a fracas at the Dhar house. We heard loud noises, profanities and curses. Pran Nath was shouting aloud, calling for help. I rushed, fearing someone was hurt or seriously ill. The clamour was coming from their back yard. It was a macabre sight. Pran Nath was being pinned down to one of the poplar trees by two sturdy men who held him fast with his back to the tree while a third was tying him to the poplar with a rope. They were tough-looking woodcutters, with muscular arms and thickset calloused hands. The victim was struggling to free himself, kicking his legs about and hurling abuse at them while they went about their business of strapping him to the tree as if he were an inanimate object. There were two other men cutting down another poplar, one holding a thick rope fastened to the tree near its top and the second bringing down his axe on the trunk. Pran Nath's wife watched the humiliation of her husband from the door of her house, wringing her hands helplessly, not knowing what to do and whether to call anyone for help. Girdhari Lal was standing nearby, his back resting against another poplar, his arms folded across his chest, watching the proceedings, unruffled.

"Stop. Why are you tying him to the tree?" I shouted at the woodcutters.

"Because he is getting in the way and preventing us from cutting down the poplars for which his brother here has taken an advance from me. We have no choice but to tie him up, so we can go about our business unhindered. Look, I do not feel good about this but I have hired and paid for the labour already. I cannot go on waiting; we have five poplars to cut and that is going to take some doing," one of them, who was in command, explained.

"Aren't you ashamed of what you are doing? How dare you

humiliate him like this? It is cruel and criminal." I reprimanded him and shouted at his mates to stop felling the poplar.

Pointing towards Girdhari Lal, he replied, "We are acting on instructions from this gentleman who claims to own the place. We have paid him an advance for the trees. It is he who needs to explain; we are only doing our job. It is he who should be ashamed." The man was brusque.

"He did not ask you to tie his brother to the tree," I quipped.

"Yes, he did, when this gentleman got in the way."

"But this is common property between the two. You cannot touch a blade of grass here without the permission of both of them. The one whom you paid for the trees does not even live here. If you do not stop I will call the police." I threatened them.

They stopped and threw up their arms in frustration. Pran Nath, wild with anger and burning with shame, extricated himself. He had a squint, inherited from his father. His one eye seemed to look at me in gratitude, the other at his brother in hatred. But he did not utter a word as he shuffled towards the house, his shirt torn near the collar, his hair ruffled, his feet bare, his chappals lying in disarray near the tree. Girdhari Lal, looking the villain and shying his gaze away from me, slinked away like a cat and disappeared inside the house. Mrs. Pran Nath, a picture of grief, sighed aloud in relief and rushed towards her husband, holding him by his arm. The poplar tree that was being hewed down was left with a big gash, oozing sap like blood from a wound. The woodcutters assembled their paraphernalia of ropes, axes and wooden pegs. They left in anger, shouting after Girdhari Lal that they would come later to get their money back along with damages. Pran Nath limped inside the house like a wounded animal to his lair. He was too shocked and traumatized to speak.

Overwhelmed by the experience, I returned home and sat thinking. Poor old Devinder Nath must never have imagined this terrible eventuality when he planted the poplars. The saplings had grown over the years into large trees boasting beautiful white barks with dark speckles and stripes and shiny serrated heart-shaped foliage that seemed to make a statement. The trunks had been strung together with a barbed wire and made a formidable fence along the boundary. How much would Girdhari Lal profit from the sale of a few poplars? It certainly could not have been for the money they would fetch because that would not be substantial. Cutting the trees down would not only ruin the look of the yard but also cause a breach in the fence. Was he testing his brother's nerve? Was it an assertion that he, being an equal owner, was at liberty to do what he liked with the property? In that case, it was a weird scheme. Getting his brother tied to the tree was brazen and brutal.

Nobody knows what transpired behind the doors of that cheerless house that took the two warring brothers in its lap, that morning after the tragic incident. There were no immediate aftershocks, not a word, not a murmur from there. It resumed its outward sepulchral calm even as there must have been raging storms in the minds of the occupants.

We never saw Girdhari Lal again. No one knows when he returned to Bombay. Was it sometime in the afternoon or during the dead of the night? Nor did Pran Nath Dhar ever discuss the shocking episode with any one. He was too proud and too shy, too private and too reticent to share his anguish or seek counsel. But he grew morose after the incident and more withdrawn than before. His stoop became pronounced, his tread slowed, and he seemed lost in thought when we crossed each other, sometimes returning my greetings in a low mumble, sometimes ignoring them altogether. He was not known for dressing in style but now he was even more careless. His thick graying hair looked more unruly than before. Often, when he returned from work, his short stocky figure would lumber slowly towards the gate of his house where he would hesitate a little, as if uncertain whether to go in or not, as if it were a stranger's house. We always knew him as an introvert who rarely conversed with his neighbors or shared a joke or spoke on topics serious or trivial. Even a comment on the weather was as remote from him as a smile. But the drastic change in his demeanor was there for all to see. His wife too kept completely to herself, too aloof to strike even an across-the-fence bonhomie with the ladies of the neighbourhood.

We never again saw the couple seated together near the window of their first floor room overlooking their lawn, which used to be their only pastime, and we saw little of their son and daughter except when they walked out of the gate on their way to school and back. It was their family trait to remain detached and insulated from others around them.

Several weeks passed and we forgot about the fracas in their backyard till one morning Pran Nath's son came running. This was probably the first time he had entered our premises. He looked terror-stricken, his hands trembling, pupils wide, mouth frothing, cheeks flushed from the panting.

"Please, doctor uncle, can you come to our place?" His tone was desperate.

"What happened?" I asked.

"Father hanged himself," he said in a tremulous voice, "please, we need help."

This was the first time any one from the family had asked us for anything. It was quite early and I was still in my night clothes. I rushed to their house and was led to a small room upstairs. Pran Nath's body lay on the floor on a white bed sheet. Around his neck was a deep mark of the rope with which he had hanged himself. The rope seemed no different from the one with which the woodcutters had tried to tie him to the poplar. His eyes were open, the one with the squint slanted, as if accusingly, at his sobbing wife, the other looking straight at the beam to which the rope had been tied.

I was dumfounded, totally at a loss for words.

"How did this happen?"

"He had an argument with mother last night." It was the daughter who spoke. She was around sixteen and quite in control of her emotions.

"What was it about?" I asked

"You know, uncle died last month," she said as if it were a mundane event, and looked at her father's corpse rather severely.

"Do you mean Girdhari Lal is dead?" I asked in surprise and horror.

"Yes."

This came as a stunning shock—the death of two brothers within a month of each other. "Oh, I am so sorry. What did he die of?"

"He had a brain tumor. He died a week after surgery."

"Did your father know about the tumor?" I asked.

"Yes, we all knew," she replied, again looking uneasily at the corpse of her father, "but father never believed him. He thought it was fiction, just a ruse that uncle employed for emotional blackmail.

I wish we had believed him. All this could have been averted."

I suddenly realized why Girdhari Lal had been in a blinding hurry to settle the property dispute with his brother.

"How appalling!" I could not hide my sorrow.

"My dad was terribly angry with his brother after the tree episode. He would froth and fume at the mention of his name. But when the news of uncle's death came, he became remorseful and sunk rapidly into depression. He wanted to attend the funeral but did not gather the courage to face the family in Bombay. He blamed himself for his brother's illness, as if it was he who had planted the tumor in his brain. Day after day, after he was home from work, he would harp on the same subjects—the property dispute, the tree episode, the brain tumor and the death of his brother. He remained mired in guilt and shame and never let go of a chance to accuse mother for all that had happened, tormenting and taunting her as if she were a witch who had worked a spell on him and his brother." She stopped when her mother cast a disapproving look at her.

"You did not seek help from anyone?" I asked. "I sensed he was low whenever we crossed each other on the road, but never imagined it would come to this. I wish you had told me. We might have been able to prevent this tragedy."

"It happened so fast. Father moved into this room ten days back. He ate little and slept alone, not letting mother come near. Last night he had another tiff with her. He refused to eat his dinner and said he was not feeling well and wanted to be left alone. Knowing him to be an early riser, when we found the door still bolted from inside this morning, we knew something was wrong. We knocked, and knocked again. There was no response. We broke in. To our utter horror, we found him hanging from the ceiling. We did not know what to do. I cut the rope with a knife while my mother and brother held the body and laid it down here. I hope we did not do anything illegal."

"I think not," I tried to reassure her.

Mrs. Pran Nath, sobbing uncontrollably, her face contorted with grief, spoke for the first time, "He never listened to us. He was always reserved, always kept his thoughts and feelings to himself, and never sought favours from any one, not even from his family. We did not realize he was planning to kill himself."

"I would never imagine he was capable of suicide," I said.

"He was a very sensitive person and loved his brother," the daughter replied.

I did not know what to say.

"What now?" I asked.

"We do not want a post-mortem or a protracted police investigation. The whole world will know, tongues will wag, and the police will make our life impossible. Our future is in peril and the family name too," pleaded the daughter poignantly.

Yes, the family name for all it was worth! It sounded bizarre after what had transpired during the last few months. What was there in the family to be proud of, to defend? The Dhars were genteel, unobtrusive and quiet but that did not prevent the coarseness of human character from surfacing at the slightest provocation, did not stop a brother getting bound to a tree by another, nor of a fraternal war culminating in tragic suicide. The pettiness that lies deep within us defies lineage and upbringing. It defies reason.

"Let us see what we can do," I said and returned home to confer with my father.

Being a man of law, he advised that the police must be informed even as we agreed that nothing ever came out of police investigations in such cases except harassment and humiliation of the bereaved by the officials. He put in a word with the police officer to not delay the cremation and prolong the pain and the agony of the family. The officer obliged and there was no inquest.

The funeral ceremony took place the same evening. There was a small gathering—some neighbors and a few close relatives. The ceremonial bath, before the journey to the cremation ground, was arranged on the back verandah. It was still an hour and a half to sunset, and the poplars in the backyard that the senior Dhar had planted twenty years earlier, cast an eerie pattern of shadows on the dead body and the assembly, as if in a final statement.

I chanced to look at the poplar that had received a big gash from the axe on that tragic morning several months earlier. The wound had healed. All one could see was a ragged scar on which fine moss was building, as if to hide the shame of the family.

2

THE GURU'S LAST WISH

It was a Sunday afternoon in November. I was driving my Ambassador, on way to Habba Kadal, the famous second bridge on the Vitasta. The window panes were drawn up and an icy draft sneaked in to send shivers down my spine and legs even as I was bundled in an overcoat, a woolen muffler and a karakuli cap. It had snowed a couple of days earlier. The movement of vehicles had turned the potholes and the ditches into pools of slush. I drove slowly to avoid splashing the pedestrians.

Nannaji, waiting on the pavement near the bridge, saw me approaching. I braked to let him in. We drove across the bridge. He asked me to park near the fire station a few hundred yards down. From there, we started walking the distance to his home at Drabiyar.

I had been invited to lunch by my former school teacher, Pandit Gopi Nath Drabu. I had never been to his house before. Nannaji, his son, now led the way through a maze of narrow lanes that got narrower and darker, with houses on either side rising three to four storeys, their balconies almost kissing each other. Some of the houses had *breirkanis*, the attics where cats sunned themselves and children played ghost games. Master Gopi Nath Drabu had told me that Drabiyar got the name after the Drabu clan, settled there several hundred years earlier.

This was an invitation that I had been postponing week after week. I had been Master Gopi Nath's favourite pupil. Now, I was his physician. He taught me at the Rangteng High School located on the bank of the Vitasta. On clear days he loved to take classes in the courtyard, under the blue sky with the sun shining bright. He was a great lover of nature and believed that open sunlight lifted spirits and made studies enjoyable. He taught us English—prose, poetry, grammar and other complexities of the language. Of a mild temperament, he hardly ever rebuked any student and never carried the cane that other teachers employed liberally on our palms, backs and bottoms. He was of lean build and medium height, always upright in stance, and wore a white turban, a churidar and an achkan that suited him well. He looked handsome in his metal-rimmed glasses that settled comfortably on his high nose. A thin film of fluid in his left eye and a drop hanging at the inner canthus, which he frequently wiped away with his handkerchief, gave him a unique liquid appeal. His benign charm and affable demeanor stood in sharp contrast to some of the other teachers that we had to reckon with—the fire-spitting Keshav Nath, the stern-looking Prem Nath with a tongue-in-cheek tic, and the short and stocky Jia Lal whose left hand fell heavy and hard on our cheeks at the slightest impropriety. Master Gopi Nath Drabu stole our hearts with his soft speech, bewitching smile and gentle manners.

But, that was not all as far as I was concerned, for he was most favourably disposed towards me. There was a reason, though. He was always on the look-out for, what he called, a boy with promise, whom he would like to groom specially. We had three sections in each grade, thirty students in each section. The three form masters would sit together and negotiate the distribution of students between the three sections according to their rank in the previous examination. When I passed my eighth grade and topped, Master Gopi Nath, one of the three form masters of the ninth grade, cut a deal with the other two. If I was placed in his section, he would accept the remaining boys of any rank.

As a first step towards improving my English language skills, Master Gopi Nath asked me to write my journal every day. It was difficult in the beginning and I lost much of my play time fulfilling this task. He would reject mediocre writing and make me rewrite the journal if he was not satisfied. I often ran to my older siblings and, sometimes to my father, for the right words and expressions. In a few weeks I settled into the practice and the strain eased. He read my journal religiously, often nodding and smiling approvingly, and proudly showed me off to other teachers, even commending my diary to Master Afzal, a tyrant who taught history and often caned students for failing to answer questions to his satisfaction. Master Afzal had an obsession with dates of major historical events and wanted each one of us to memorize them. He was rather poor in English and in his spare time at school he took lessons in the language from Master Gopi Nath. Now that he got to read my journal, I became his surrogate teacher. As a reward, he passed on his rod to me, affording me the special privilege of caning the students who failed to answer his questions. That was the worst affront to my classmates. They burned with envy even as I generally let them off with light strokes, for they preferred a lashing at the hands of Master Afzal to my leniency. Within days, they started memorizing the dates so well that the cane became redundant and I breathed a sigh of relief.

Master Gopi Nath revelled in my presence in the classroom. While teaching he looked at me, as if there was no other student in the class. I had to reciprocate with full attention and nod in understanding and approval. He often fired questions at students and when they failed to answer he turned to me, sure of a correct answer every time. He would bring along his five-year-old son, Nannaji, and seat him by my side, while the class went on, in the belief that some of my perceived intelligence would rub off on him. I basked in his attention and admiration. Taking care of his son was a privilege I enjoyed.

It was the same Nannaji who now accompanied me to his home. I had lost contact with my teacher and his son after I passed matriculation and joined Sri Pratap College. Though I had secured the sixth place in the university finals, he felt rather let down; he would have liked me to top the list. I moved on after another two years to pursue medicine at Patiala and Delhi. By the time I returned with a postgraduate degree, the first medical college had been established in Srinagar and, soon after, I was on the faculty. Meanwhile, Nannaji had managed to scrape through his B.A. and secured a clerical post in the Accountant General's office. He had not come up to the expectations of his father.

Nearly five years after I started my medical practice, Master Gopi Nath sought my consultation. I practiced at Chotta Bazar, hardly a mile from Drabiyar. We met after seventeen years. He had retired and was much changed and rundown, but the unmistakable liquid look had stayed with him. He seemed much older than his years and quite weak, but managed to embrace me tightly. It was an emotional reunion.

Master Gopi Nath had been experiencing difficulty swallowing food for some time now. In the beginning it was easier to swallow soft food and liquids, but anything eaten in haste caused him discomfort. He choked at times and adapted himself to eating small frequent meals, easing the food down with swigs of water. During the previous few weeks, however, even liquids were becoming difficult to swallow. He had lost weight appreciably and become a pale shadow of his former self. Medications did not provide any relief. X-rays, performed several months earlier, had not revealed any abnormality.

The symptoms suggested a progressive obstruction in the foodpipe. I detected a node in his neck. This was a sinister sign, possibly a metastasis from cancer in his food pipe. I was aware of the high incidence of this monstrous disease among Kashmiris. I had lost an uncle to it when I was in my teens. Now it was my beloved teacher.

Master Gopi Nath Drabu was admitted to my ward in the hospital. Further examinations and tests confirmed metastasized esophageal cancer. This was the age of conservative medicine, the age of philosophical resignation to the inevitable, the age of passive submission to cruel destiny. Patients were sent home to die—no heroics, no experimentation.

I explained the prognosis to my revered teacher. He may have grasped the full import of what I was trying to tell him—that there was nothing that could be done—but he was not ready to accept that

I, his star pupil, would not be able to alleviate his distress.

"I am sure you will make it easy for me. I do not care how long I live; if I could just swallow it would be a great relief," he pleaded.

His faith in me was implacable—the faith of a guru in his disciple. That is when I thought of a feeding tube and discussed with him a relatively simple procedure that would entail a small surgical incision in the upper abdomen to allow the placement of a tube inside his stomach.

"I know you will do the best for me," he said, and gave me his permission without a second thought.

We started intravenous infusions to boost his nutrition. I arranged for a blood transfusion and roped in my surgical colleagues. He returned home ten days later, fitted with a feeding tube through which he himself administered his feeds. I explained how to care for the skin around the tube and how to hide the tube under his clothing.

Over the succeeding weeks, he became adept in selfcare and often came to see me in my consulting chamber. He gained a little weight and looked somewhat healthier. People marvelled at his seeming recovery. He told me that he went about his daily routine without revealing the secret of the feeding tube to any one except his family.

It was during one of these visits that he invited me to his home for dinner. I kept refusing the invitation under one pretext or other. With the certain knowledge that he was not going to last more than a few months, I did not have the heart to be his dinner guest while he suffered. Besides, I knew he was a person of modest means. Teachers were poorly paid. I did not like the idea of straining his family budget. I remembered one of my teachers in my primary school who was so hard up, he could not afford to buy a pair of new shoes.

Master Gopi Nath felt offended when I declined his invitation, possibly for the fifth time. Was he a pariah, he asked? That is when I promised him that I would certainly eat at his place. He was happy.

"Let it be this coming Sunday," he suggested.

"No, I will eat with you after the first snowfall of the season," I promised.

His appetite had started to fade, and he was again losing weight and strength. The cancer was spreading, the node in the neck was getting bigger, and more nodes were surfacing. From the way he was going downhill, I felt he could not last more than a few weeks. It was early September and the first snow generally appeared in December. That was a long time away.

As if reading my thoughts, he asked, "Are you waiting to visit me after I am gone?"

I was red with shame and fumbled for an answer. "I will certainly lunch with you and have fish," I said reassuringly.

"You can have it tomorrow. My wife cooks fish with a passion." There was gentle persuasion in his eyes, a pleading note in his voice.

"Father says that fish should not be eaten in this season when they spawn. We have the whole winter ahead of us, and there is nothing like fish after a fresh snowfall. That is when I relish it most. Fish and brown rice," I replied, and at once regretted why I had mentioned brown rice.

He must have prayed for an early snowfall more than for his life. That year, it snowed in November. He wanted to call on me personally to remind me of my promise but he had grown too weak and the snow was thick on the roads. He sent his son instead. It was Friday. I said I would lunch with them on Sunday. That is how Nannaji was waiting for me at the bridge to lead me to his home.

It was a great welcome. My teacher's eyes lit up as soon as I entered the low-ceiling, small, almost claustrophobic room where he lay on a mattress in a corner near the window. Too weak to stand, he sat up and opened his arms wide to hug me. He took out the *kangri* from under his *pheron* and passed it on to me. "Your hands are cold, come warm them." Then to his son, "Get a blanket, the one which you bought last week, and drape it on his legs."

I sat at the balcony window near his bed as he leaned on the bolster, facing me. He was a picture of ecstasy. He wiped the drop that had collected at the corner of his eye.

It was one of the most memorable lunches I have ever had. I marvelled at the effort that had gone into it. He had sent Nannaji to Sopore, thirty miles west of Srinagar to procure the fabled Sopore trout. His wife had cooked the fish with great love and care with the right mixture of spices for this special recipe of fish with lotus roots.

And there was brown rice! That was a scarce commodity after the green revolution supplanted the brown variety for higher yielding ones. His son had gone to great lengths to procure it from a friend in Ganderbal, another twelve miles to the north. It was overwhelming. I felt guilty and irresponsible for having mentioned fish and brown rice so casually and carelessly when he extended the invitation. I never believed then that this dinner would actually come to pass. This was a burden of gratitude that my teacher heaped on me, never to be repaid.

The window overlooked the lanes and the neighbouring houses. There was snow on the ground, snow on the roofs, snow on the adobe walls, and snow on the trees and bushes. But everything else was warm—the reception, the *kangri*, the food, and the warmest hearts that beat with contentment as I ate and relished dish after dish, course after course.

Master Gopi Nath pressed me to eat another and yet another piece of fish as if he was enjoying it himself. His son sat near to pass on the salad, his wife making trips to the kitchen to fetch new courses of lotus root, spinach, pickles and more fish. It was a delicious, love-laden lunch.

"It makes me feel odd and uncomfortable that all of you are waiting on me while I eat. Why can't you join me?" I asked.

"Let us wallow in the joy of watching you eat. I lost taste for food long back and, since you introduced the feeding tube, it is immaterial what I put inside my stomach. I could be eating saw dust for all I care. But now, vicariously, I taste and relish each item as I watch you eat."

My beloved teacher was a satisfied man that day. He watched me with amusement and love, as he sat there, debilitated and weak, the film of liquid in the left eye shining in the reflection of the midday sun that found its way inside through a narrow stretch of the sky between the houses.

Lunch was followed by tea spiced with almonds and saffron, cinnamon and cardamom.

We talked nostalgically about school days and his eyes shone with pride when I acknowledged that he had played a great part in shaping my career and life. He did not regret anything in life but wished Nannaji had done better than he had. His wife looked at me as a savior, hardly aware of the proximity of death.

It was time to take leave. I moved nearer to him and took his hands in mine but he pulled me closer and hugged me again. He must have drawn on the last vestiges of his strength to hold me so tightly. It was some time before he let me go.

"Now I can die in peace. I will take this image of my favourite student with me, as a last testimony that my life did not go waste. You are my best medal," he said in his feeble voice.

I felt humbled. His eyes followed me as I left the room. Out on the street, I turned to look back at the house and at the window where I had sat. Master Gopi Nath had moved from his bed to the window to watch me leave. I waved and he waved back, as he wiped a bead from his eye.

3
PRICE OF A LAMB

We were visiting a friend in his new house at Natipora, a fledgling suburb on the Srinagar-Chrar highway. The road was rough and replete with potholes and ditches. It forked into smaller lanes inside the new settlement. Here, we drove lazily, stopping at places to inquire where our friend lived, passing through dirt paths that merged imperceptibly with large uninhabited tracts of land. Close to our destination, we were slowed by a large herd of sheep that blocked the long narrow path to the house. The sheep refused to budge. I honked to scatter them, but they huddled together and tied themselves in knots, raising clouds of dust. We were so close to our destination but here we were caught in this mess from which an escape seemed difficult any time soon. In my impatience, I continued to drive at a snail's pace, expecting the herd to separate and allow us to pass through. Suddenly, a lanky lad appeared from nowhere, as if by magic—a sun-burnt face with a shock of unruly hair, wearing a loose striped shirt and grey shalwar, a long slender willow stick in hand.

He came running and hurling invectives. "Have you no eyes, you heartless Batta? You nearly crushed my lamb to death!"

We were shocked by the unexpected verbal onslaught and the sobriquet. Leela, sitting to my left, held my arm, urging me not to return the compliment. As soon as I stopped the car, the fuming protestor caught up with us and tried to force open the door on her side. I moved out of the car to stop him and to find out the reason for his outburst. And there, right in front of the car bumper was a little lamb, struggling to stand. I picked it up and put it down again. It limped. It had sustained a fracture in the left hind leg.

"I am sorry I failed to see the little creature from inside the car. It must have been very close to the bumper. It is not my fault entirely; you let the sheep block this lane. I was driving very slowly; I could not have waited here for ever."

"Don't you see they are dumb little animals, not humans? Could you not wait a minute to let them pass? You act as if this entire place belongs to you and you have the right to run over animals and humans alike." His small eyes flashed, getting narrower and sharper in their deep sockets. The dirty brown hair stood up as he jerked his head and waved the stick in anger. He could not have been more than fifteen.

I fumbled for an answer. "Well, there is nothing we can do about it now. What has happened has happened. Let us not make it a big issue. Let us resolve this small matter here."

"How can you call it a small matter? You have disabled this innocent creature!" he retorted.

"Come on, I am a doctor. I can set the fracture of this lamb if you let me, and also compensate you for the distress I have caused."

I was conciliatory.

"You don't realize what you have done. My innocent lamb is maimed for life. Can it ever walk and run about like healthy sheep, ever climb a hill, ever be the same as before?" He was arguing like a lawyer, building up his case.

"All right, why don't you sell it to me? What could be the weight of this lamb? I will pay you at the going rate!"

No sooner had I uttered those last words, I realized my impudence.

"No, I am not interested in selling my lamb. You claim to be a doctor, but do not seem to know what the price of a life is. This tiny creature is not mutton for sale in a butcher shop. This is a tender life that you nearly throttled, and now you want to pay for it as if it were a dead weight. How can you be so bereft of feeling?"

I felt cornered, and fumbled for an answer. These arguments, so cogently put forth, were unexpected from a village lad. I wanted to resolve this issue, compensate him or even buy the little helpless creature from him. I was willing to take the injured lamb to a vet or set its fracture myself. There had to be some means of settling this, or someone who could intercede and rid me of this quarrelsome brat.

Leela looked on helplessly, hoping for a quick solution. She came out of the car and addressed him, "Please state your price, take the money, and let us go. We will carry this lamb with us and take care of it."

"How can you take this lamb, Madam? Do you Battas have a heart? Do you possess any knowledge about rearing cattle? It is still a baby sucking at its mother's teats; I can not let it die under your care. Who knows, you might even make a hearty meal of it." He was irascible, irritating, irreconcilable.

She maintained her composure in the face of his tirade. It was clear he was gunning for trouble and not interested in settling the problem. He was on the offensive as soon as he knew we were Pandits, betrayed by the saffron mark on our foreheads and the traditional *dejhour* dangling from Leela's ears. A counter-offensive would have been useless and could land us in danger as it does in this part of the world if you are pitted against a member of the majority community.

"Well, where do we go from here? You are making too much of this minor incident and we have important business to attend to. Since you are not interested in resolving this issue in an amicable manner you should register a case with the police and let the law take its course. Or, speak your price, take the cash and take the lamb as well and deal with it the way you see fit. But for god's sake, let us bring this matter to a close."

Whether it was a chivalrous response to a lady's plea or the mention of police, he seemed to mellow and said, "All right, if you want someone else to settle this between us, go do it."

I looked around. We were not far from the main street and the market place. I suggested we drive there and find some one who might give us an idea what this injured little lamb was worth.

"No, the car will stay here. I cannot trust you. You might just drive away. I will wait here while you go and find out from whoever you like. Besides, I cannot abandon my herd here." He was unrelenting.

"Since you don't trust us, why don't you come along? Let us both walk to the market."

He agreed, and followed me, lamb in his lap. I asked Leela to stay behind. It was not long before we found a butcher's shop. The owner looked inquiringly at me.

Pointing at the lamb, I asked, "Mister, could you give us an idea how much this lamb might cost?"

"Why may you want to know the price, sir?" he asked sarcastically. "I am not interested in buying this little thing if that is what you came for."

I related the story and sought his help.

'Panditji, this lamb is just a fledgling; I have no idea what it costs. We do not buy baby sheep here. I am sorry, I cannot help you," the butcher replied brusquely.

The shepherd lad was amusing himself at my discomfiture. But having come thus far, I was in no mood to give up.

"You could weigh it on the scales and let us have some idea of the price," I persisted.

"No sir, this is not my calling. It is forbidden to weigh a baby lamb. It is against our religion. Why do you ask me to weigh this innocent little lamb and heap your sins on me?" He was censorious.

The lad was grinning mischievously, enjoying the exchange.

By this time, an inquisitive crowd had gathered around us. I felt very awkward, having to explain the problem again in an attempt to seek support from some quarter. This incident was degenerating into an ugly farce. We were getting late for the evening clinic. Our patients would be waiting. The friend we had come to visit would be wondering why we had not turned up. He was so near, yet so remote from my mind now.

The crowd started inching closer, commenting disparagingly:

"How cruel of Panditji to have run over an innocent creature!"

"How callous of him to offer money for the weight of a poor lamb!"

"Can there be a price for a life?"

"No, not at all," the crowd replied in unison, shaking their heads from side to side.

"And he claims he is a doctor," an aggressive looking youth from the mob shouted, eyeing me menacingly.

"They think they can trample on us as they used to in the past, these Battas. They must face retribution," declared another, as if I were a criminal caught in the act of committing a heinous crime.

The crowd was surging, emotions rising, and the threshold for an outburst getting closer. Yet, this was not uncommon—this incitement, this vilification, this ugly profiling of Pandits as usurpers, tyrants. It was the fabled lion and the lamb story—fishing for any imagined or contrived excuse to harass and to humiliate. Had I belonged to their faith, the shepherd boy would have felt sorry for letting his sheep block my way. He would have been reprimanded by the same people for making an issue out this. But here I was, heckled and held to ransom, while fear wrenched my wife's heart as she waited near the car.

Leela could not stand the suspense any longer and walked over to join me. She sensed my exasperation and the physical danger I was in. She was there to restrain me from losing my cool. It would not take much provocation for the mob, that had now gathered, to go out of control. An unwitting remark could set off fireworks and magnify this into an all-too-familiar communal incident. We had to get out of the situation somehow. The fate of the lamb had become irrelevant except as an excuse for the crowd to entertain itself by harassing us.

"Ha! Ha! The lady is here to shield him. Battas are known to hide behind the saris of their women when they find themselves in a difficult situation," a skull-capped, middle-aged hooligan hurled the last salvo.

I looked him hard in the eye, ready to go after him, but Leela squeezed my arm again to restrain me. The crowd fell silent in anticipation of a flare up when a short, thickset, balding, bearded man broke the ring, came near and looked at me in recognition.

"Salaam, Doctor Sahib. What a pleasant surprise! How did you find time to grace our neighborhood?" he greeted me with courtesy.

I could not place him, nor was I in a mood to explain my predicament yet again, even as I heaved a sigh of relief on finding a sympathetic face in the crowd.

"Salaam," I replied, raising my hands in a helpless gesture and pointing at the lamb in the arms of the boy who held it high for everyone to see, looking accusingly at me for having committed this act of great barbarity.

All eyes turned towards the object of sympathy as the lamb gave out a loud plaintive bleat, echoed by its mother from the herd afar. The crowd guffawed.

I addressed the stranger, "I hurt his lamb by accident and would be glad to compensate for it, but this young lad has made it a life-and-death issue."

Scanning the crowd in one wide sweep of his puffy eyes, he thundered, "What is this tamasha all about?" and addressing the lad, "why are you holding Doctor Sahib up? The sky has not fallen because your lamb got hurt. Accidents do happen. If he is ready to square up with you, why don't you accept his offer? Is there something the matter with you that needs to be looked into? In that case, he is the doctor to go to, for he treats crazy people. Ask your price and let us settle this. Take the money and give him the lamb. Do you understand?"

His eyes took another broad sweep of the crowd. "Does any one here have any objection?"

A long silence ensued.

I looked at this divine apparition with gratitude, still unable to place him, Leela by my side looking away from so many peering eyes, the shepherd crestfallen, the crowd waiting for the next move.

"I am sure they have patients waiting in their clinic. Don't waste any more of their time. Let me tell you something, young lad. When you are married and your wife goes into labour and your baby refuses to come out, this noble lady will cut open her tummy and deliver you your lamb, safe and sound."

The last statement threw the whole crowd into a roar of laughter. Suddenly the explosive situation changed into one of hilarity, as if by magic.

People nodded in agreement.

The boy's face fell. He froze to the ground, looking indecisively at the lamb in his lap, patting it nervously.

"Come on, state your price," my messiah roared at the boy.

The boy gazed at him speechless,

Giving the boy a severe look, he continued, "This lamb must weigh nearly a kilo and a half. Mutton sells at sixty a kilo. Take twice the price and go home." Then, he faced me and said, "Doctor Sahib, please pay him and take the lamb. You must be getting late to work."

The crowd remained silent. The judgment had been delivered. There would be no appeal.

"It is a fair bargain, Rehman Sahib," a man from the crowd put the stamp of finality on the judgment.

I lost no time, counted the money, handed it over to the boy, thanked my deliverer profusely, took the lamb gingerly in my hands and walked back to the car, Leela, a picture of relief, by my side.

A part of the crowd followed us as we walked towards the car. The herd had not moved and still blocked the road. We got inside the car. Handing the lamb over to Leela, I switched on the ignition. The engine roared and I waited for the shepherd to lead the sheep away and clear the road. He cast a rueful look at me before he whistled and drove the herd aside.

As we started, my eyes caught sight of the lamb looking at me with its gentle eyes. I let the engine idle, took the lamb from Leela, alighted from the car and hailed the shepherd lad.

"I am sorry for what happened. You are right; we cannot take care of this innocent creature. Here, take it to its mother and look after its leg," I said as I offered the lamb back to him.

He was bewildered and looked at me in disbelief, not certain whether he should take the lamb.

"Take it," I said and thrust the animal in his arms.

Before he could speak a word, I got into the car, pressed my foot on the accelerator and drove off.

Looking through the rear view mirror, I saw the lad smiling for the first time, and the crowd waving at our retreating car. But, I could not see Rehman Sahib. He was gone as mysteriously as he had appeared.

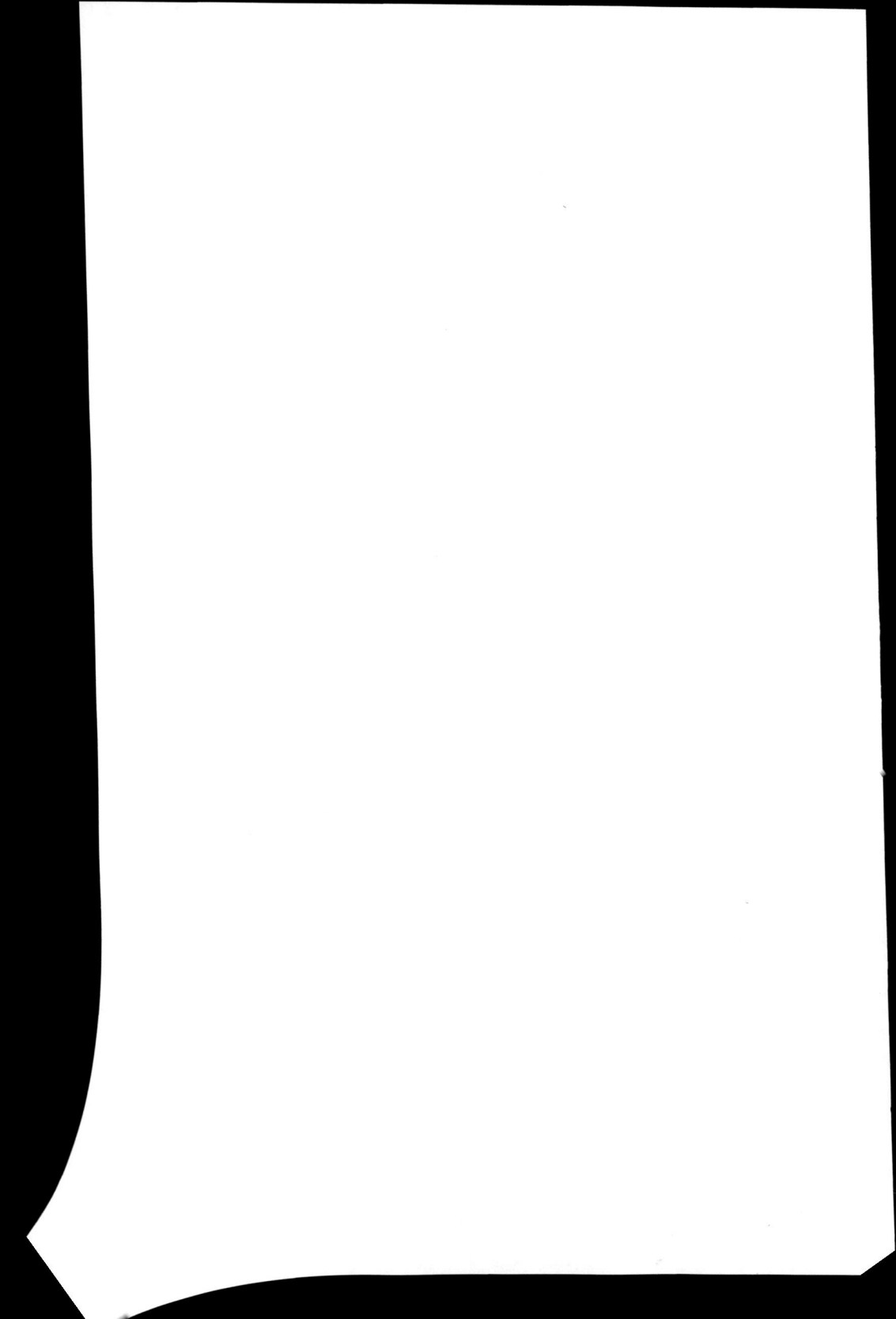

4

FAITH AND FRENZY

Pandit Shyam Lal, a retired middle rung official of the Public Works Department, lived at Chattabal in downtown Srinagar. On a cold afternoon of February 1990, when Kashmir was gripped by terrorism, he sat sipping tea with his wife. The atmosphere inside the house was one of gloom and foreboding. Shyam Lal and his wife were debating whether they should stay behind or, like many other Kashmiri Pandit families, leave the valley for the unknown terrains of exile.

The debate went thus: The situation here is explosive. Terrorists have killed many innocent Kashmiri Pandits. They are targeting our youth in particular. We cannot be faulted for sending our children away for some time. Let us hope they will find refuge somewhere and return when the situation improves. There is nobody in Jammu or Delhi, that we could call our own and who could provide us a roof over our heads, in case we too decide to move. Hopefully, that should not be necessary since we are ordinary civilians without any party or political affiliations. We have always led a quiet and simple life, in complete harmony with our Muslim neighbours. We hardly need to step outdoors except to buy groceries, and we do not have any enemies. The neighbours were supportive when we sent our sons away, and we have not received any threats from anyone. Why should we abandon our home and leap into the unknown? Let us watch the situation and wait before we take a step we may regret.

Just when they seemed to settle on this line of thinking, there was a knock on the door. Shyam Lal rose to check. He had barely opened it a chink when he was pushed back. He staggered and the turban fell off his head. Attired in leather jackets and jeans, four young men forced entry into the house. They were rough and gruff, and seemed in desperate haste. The couple was completely taken by surprise and, before they could remonstrate, the intruders started searching the house frantically, going from one room to another, turning the furniture upside down, and looking under the beds, behind the doors and inside the bathroom. One of them ran up the stairs to the attic and returned to tell the others that he found no trace of the quarry. Another, pointing a knife at Shyam Lal and looking at him menacingly, growled, "Where are your sons?"

Shyam Lal's heart skipped a beat, his breathing ceased momentarily and his speech froze, even as he thanked god that he had sent his sons away just in time.

It seemed like an eternity.

"Speak, you old villain; where are your sons hiding?" The knife came closer to his chest

"We sent them away. They must be in Jammu." He could barely speak.

"So they ran away, eh, before we could lay our hands on them, bloody spies! We will seek them out wherever they are. Meanwhile, you need to come with us to answer some questions, old rascal."

Shyam Lal slumped on the floor, begging them to leave him alone. His wife folded her hands for mercy when they seized hold of him and started dragging him out of the house. His arm hurt badly and he squealed in pain. They shouted at him to shut up or they would kill him. Realizing that there was no point in resisting, he stood up and let them lead him out, looking back helplessly at his wife. She picked his turban from the floor and shuffled towards the door to pass it on to her husband. They snatched it from her, flung it on the verandah and closed the door behind them. She was left alone, wailing and weeping, not knowing where to turn to for help. The neighbours watched from behind half-closed windows as the desperadoes blindfolded him, pushed him into a waiting Ambassador and sped away.

The car zigzagged through side streets and narrow lanes and stopped after about fifteen minutes. When they removed his blindfold, he found himself in a deserted willow field. The trees stood in rows with their bare branches touching each other in a fantastic pageant. The sky was overcast but the trees were full of promise, their pink buds ready to unfold in the first flush of spring. The kidnappers lit a cigarette each and the interrogation began in earnest through spirals and jets of smoke let off from their mouths and nostrils.

The militant flashing the knife took the lead. He was the tallest and seemed to command authority.

"Now, tell us, you old devil, where have you hidden your sons? We will spare you if you tell us the truth, otherwise we can be very nasty," he threatened.

Shyam Lal looked at their stern faces for the first time. They were between twenty and twenty five years old, bareheaded, sporting short hair and cropped beards, speaking chaste Kashmiri.

"I swear by god, they are not here. But, why do you ask? Have they done anything wrong?"

The militant slapped him hard on his face. "Do not pretend ignorance, you bloody Indian agent. We know that all of you Pandits are in league with the police and the military. You spy on us and inform them about our movements and activities. You are the enemies of Jihad."

"But we do not even know you. How can we inform on you? I see you as nice young men who should be in school rather than intimidating old men, pointing knives at them, dragging them out of their homes for no reason," he replied, looking his tormentor in the eye.

"You will get to know us soon, you wily old fox. We have information that your sons are around. They were spotted here last week."

"Yes, they were here until four days ago. By my honour, we are innocent. We have nothing to do with the military or the police."

"As if you infidels have any honour," the leader spat at him and guffawed. He was enjoying the experience, impressing his mates.

"Your sons were leading the agitation to get the temple reopened, were they not? You want to reclaim the temple land that belongs to us, eh?" This was from the second in command. He was referring to the Bhairav temple in Chattabal. Muslims of the mohalla had laid claim to the temple land and forced the closure of the temple. The dispute had gone on for several years and was left unresolved after the temple was locked by a court order and Pandits were stopped from praying there. In any case, the charge was irrelevant and had nothing to do with the present turmoil in Kashmir. It was the old lamb and the lion story.

"That was a long time back. The temple has been locked up for years. My sons have nothing to do with the temple dispute or with your Jihad."

"Why did your sons run to Jammu if they are innocent?"

"Because innocent folk are being hounded out and done to death. We are being forced to run away to save our lives."

That incensed the inquisitors. How dare this old wretch answer them back! They stung him with burning cigarette butts, kicked him, and slapped him harder. He winced in pain and begged to be left alone. He swore repeatedly that he and his family had nothing against them and no link whatsoever with the security agencies.

"What are you doing here when you have already sent your sons away if it is not to spy on us?"

"Yes, I have no reason to be here now. I will leave at the first opportunity if you let me go." He was bold, defiant.

"Before we do that, you have a lot more questions to answer," snarled the leader. "First, tell us which hole in Jammu your two snakes are hiding in; we have to ferret them out, cut their forked tongues and crush their poison filled heads."

"Believe me, I do not even know where they are. I have no news from them so far. We have no relatives in Jammu, no friends. They must have sought shelter in a temple or in one of the tents that the government has put up for the refugees."

"You are a liar. Your sons are informers. You are spies. You are members of the RSS. Tell us the truth and we will let you off. Hide it and we will cut off your ears."

The old man denied all allegations.

They boxed his ears and kicked his legs. He writhed in pain but did not cry.

They stripped him off his *pheron* and tore his vest and shirt. He lay crumpled on the ground.

"We will give you one last chance," the leader thundered as he kicked him again. "We have information that both your sons are in hiding here and have not left for Jammu. Tell us where they are and we will let you off."

"Kill me if you must but I have nothing more to reveal and nothing to hide," he made bold to declare.

The militants detested his audacity. They moved away towards a large willow tree and huddled into a quick conference.

Meanwhile, Shyam Lal stood up and looked around for the first time. This seemed a familiar place. He realized that it was hardly a mile from his home and that the river was quite near. There was a bridge on the river nearby which was guarded by a police picket. But that would not make any difference to him. If he shouted for help, it would be his end. He was in the jaws of death from which only some superior power could pull him out.

It took them just five minutes to negotiate his fate and pass the death sentence on him.

"We do not believe a word of what you have said. We have definite information that you and your sons are spies; that you are in league with the enemy; that you are harming the cause of Azadi. Death is a fitting punishment for these heinous crimes. We decree that you be hanged right away," the leader pronounced the judgment.

Without losing time, they set about their business. Shyam Lal made a last desperate plea while they slung a rope around a stout branch of the tree, made a noose and secured it around his neck, and stood him on a rock.

"Please let me go. Have mercy on this old man. If I die, my wife will die with me and you will have committed a double murder. Is this what your religion teaches you—to kill innocent people?"

"Don't try to teach us our religion, you infidel," the leader growled.

Invoking the intervention of Prophet Muhammad, Shyam Lal said, "I might let you know that I have great faith in the dargah at Hazratbal that houses the Prophet's sacred hair. I was a daily visitor to the dargah during the last five years of my service because I was a maintenance engineer of the sacred precincts. I believe the Prophet's holy relic will come to my rescue for he knows that I am blameless."

They ridiculed his claim, calling him a hypocrite, an old villain, an impostor who deserves death.

And then they pushed the rock away from under Shyam Lal's feet.

Instead of hanging, Shaym Lal fell down with a thud and the tree sprung back. The few leaves that still clung to the branches rained down on him in a gentle shower. He stood up immediately, gave them an I-told-you-so look, and started dusting the dirt off his clothes. He seemed unharmed and unperturbed. The militants were stunned.

Shyam Lal retained the presence of mind to seek divine intervention again, and to remind them of retribution. "Now you must believe my innocence and let me off. The holy Prophet knows it. That is why he came to my rescue. Please, do not invite his wrath by killing me."

They were mystified. The hanging fiasco made them uneasy. It was a mistake to throw the turban away, they realized. It would have come handy. But, they would not be cowed down by an infidel. How dare he curse them, this non-believer, faking faith in Prophet Muhammad in whose service they had taken up Jihad? No, this was a minor setback. They shall not be taken in by his wizardry. This man has to die, they decided.

The leader flicked open his pocket knife and started slashing him, inflicting deep cuts on his limbs. Others watched him bleed as they smoked cigarettes. The red fluid flowed down in narrow trails and congealed in strange shapes on the ground where he lay, making no movement at all, not pleading any more, accepting the inevitable. He turned pale, his breathing became shallow, almost imperceptible, his body lay haphazard on the ground like a rag.

"Om Namah Shivaya," he muttered the Vedic invocation with which he would start each day of his life, and passed out.

They rolled him over, kicked him, found him limp and lifeless and, taking him for dead, walked away.

The clouds were moving languidly. The setting sun—large and red—threw long shadows of the leafless trees, crisscrossing the field like dancing skeletons in a surreal play of light and shade. Dusk was descending fast and the birds were flitting across the sky to their nests. Shyam Lal regained consciousness. He was dazed and too weak to think or move. What was he doing in this wilderness? Where was his wife? He tried to sit up but slumped again. He collected his thoughts. Slowly, he recalled the events of the day and realized that he had survived two attempts on his life that afternoon. He was destined to live, he thought, and must wait till he recovered enough strength to walk.

The hope that stirred in his heart surged suddenly when he felt a shadow fall on him ahead of an approaching person. It was a man with a long grey beard in a *pheron* and a white skullcap. It could be a man returning from the evening nimaz, sent by the almighty to rescue him, he thought. Was it deliverance, finally?

"Please help me, brother." Shyam Lal could barely utter the words when the person halted near him.

"Why are you in this condition?" the stranger asked.

"The boys tried to hang me but the noose came loose and I was saved. Then they stabbed me repeatedly and I passed out. They must have taken me for dead. But Allah is merciful. I survived, for He wants me to live, and now He sent you to rescue me. Please be a good Muslim and arrange to take me home to my wife. She must be dying to know about my welfare." He fainted again.

"Of course I will. I will finish the unfinished business," and saying so, the stranger grabbed his arms and dragged him to the riverbank. Pushing him into the river, he yelled, "From here straight to hell, you infidel," and went his way.

Shyam Lal fell headlong into the shallow river. However, this final assault saved his life instead of drowning him. The cold water numbed his pain and stopped the hemorrhaging from the cuts and slashes. The chill caused him to shiver so strongly that he regained full consciousness. Gradually, he recovered enough strength to crawl out of the river and drag his body, heavy with his waterlogged dress, to the nearby police picket. He shouted for help and fainted again.

The discourse between Shyam Lal and his wife, that had started on that fateful afternoon in their home at Chattabal, took final shape in the dying moments of the day as he lay recovering in the hospital from a third attempt on his life. They decided to board the first bus that would take them out of the accursed valley as soon as he was declared fit to go home.

5
PREMONITION

Prem Nath ran his business from a shop in the busy and bustling shopping center at Amira Kadal in the heart of Srinagar. He was a successful cloth merchant and his sales were brisk in spite of the terrorism that had gripped Kashmir and paralyzed business. People needed clothes to wear; women were commanded to wear the burqa, men the kameez and shalwar, while the militants queued for *pherons* that served to conceal their weapons. Prem Nath loved his work and was reluctant to leave his beloved home in Jawahar Nagar, not far from his shop. Muslim shopkeepers in the vicinity asked him the awkward question: why was he staying back when his co-religionists, the Pandits, were on the run? He could not decide if it was a taunt, a veiled threat or just idle curiosity, but their inquisitiveness made him uncomfortable.

Come January 19 night, a watershed in the uprising, thousands of loudspeakers, hoisted on the domes, turrets and minarets of mosques across the length and breadth of the valley of Kashmir, boomed all at once on the denizens of the city, exhorting them to come out of their homes and seize power from the 'Indian occupational forces'. Azadi and pro-Pakistan slogans filled the air. It was a tape-recorded message played from every loud speaker at the same hour, loaded with exhortations:

"Arise O Muslims of Kashmir; throw the Kafirs out, fight the Indian dogs."

"Those who want to live in Kashmir will have to recite the Kalima."

"What do we want?"

"We want Pakistan."

"What is the meaning of Azadi"?

"La ilaha illallah."

This was an unambiguous warning to Kashmiri Pandits to quit the valley or face retribution. Most of them felt they had to run for their lives. Some had already left in the wake of the ongoing killings, but now the trickle developed into a torrent.

Prem Nath hated to even consider the prospect of deserting his home and his work. He had assiduously built his business with hard work and fair competition. He owned a modest house and led a contented life with his family. But times had changed fast. Terror had stabbed the tender hearts of Pandits. They felt besieged. Militants had gunned down a distant cousin of Prem Nath in his office a month before the terrorizing slogans rent the blue sky of the valley. Yet, and despite his family's urging, Prem Nath had not budged. However, after the dark night of January 19, his wife pressed her point again and prevailed. A compromise was reached. They would move temporarily to Jammu and watch the situation from there, but Prem Nath would return at the earliest sign of improvement.

The family departed a week later and landed at Jammu amid chaos and confusion.

***

Refugee life in Jammu was at once repugnant and intolerable for Prem Nath. The humiliation and suffering which he had to go through to get registered as a refugee was worse than the terror back home. The militants had a conviction, howsoever misplaced, that Pandits were enemies of their revolution and had to be thrown out of the valley. There was no hypocrisy there. But the officials of the relief administration, supposed to lend succor, were unfeeling and inhuman in their dealings with the refugees. The Pandits had to face horrendous bureaucratic roadblocks and delays to have their credentials verified before they could claim the meagre dole.

Every passing day was like living a hell in the tent provided to Prem Nath and his family on the outskirts of Jammu in the Muthi Migrant Camp—a brambly wasteland rife with snakes, scorpions and shadowy characters. He felt great remorse at having left his home, and lost his appetite and sleep. He missed his dear home. He missed the temple, which he would visit every morning before leaving for work. He missed his shop and his fellow shopkeepers of Amira Kadal. He dreamt of customers buying rolls of cloth at his shop. He was in despair.

Meanwhile, summer announced itself with a bang in Jammu. The sun was a fireball ready to burn the tents and their contents. The blinding dust storms that followed blew the flaps of the tents away and hot air rushed in to slap and scorch the occupants and scatter their possessions. They were caught in reveries of their dear homeland and cursed the day they left. Many lost their lives to heat strokes.

Prem Nath had not spent even a single day of his fifty six summers away from the salubrious climes of Kashmir. He grew restless and paced about most of the time during the day. During nights, he sat up in the bed or moved out of the tent into the open, unmindful that he might be bitten by a snake or a scorpion. He ate little. His deteriorating health became a matter of great concern for the family. They tried to counsel him out of his depression. After all, their family was not alone in this tragedy; there were hundreds and thousands who had left their homes in the valley and did not have even a temporary cover on their heads. They consoled him with the hope that things would improve, and that they would return home as soon as terrorism was contained and peace returned to the valley. But he was not receptive to reason or argument. He longed for his home and pined for his work. He knew that there were still a few thousand residual Pandits in the valley and some of them ran their business as before. He heard they were paying protection money to the militants. Why shouldn't he give it a try, speak to his Muslim neighbours and buy the patronage of the militant outfits to restart his life in the valley?

After a long debate, the family decided that it would be better for Prem Nath to return home than waste and wither away in exile. He would go alone and call his wife once he settled down. His sons would follow if he found the conditions congenial for their return. They looked up the *Jantri* for an auspicious date.

***

Four-and-a-half months after the exodus, an uncertain, uneasy, and unhappy Prem Nath boarded a bus to Srinagar. He sighed throughout the journey as the fellow passengers, mostly Muslims, looked at him curiously. His mind was in turmoil. Was he already persona non grata for the sin of having been absent from Kashmir for several months? He was told that the Pandits who had left the valley were called runaways who had forfeited the right to return. What explanation would he give, what face would he show? What about his house? Would he find it in order, vandalized or gutted? What about his shop; had his landlord forced entry and seized possession without his knowledge? Was his merchandise still intact? How would he tackle his neighbours, customers and fellow merchants? He rehearsed in his mind over and over again how he would answer their queries. How would he commute from the bus stand to home? Would he walk or hire a taxi? He had learned that many young men who plied taxis were in league with the militants and informed them of passengers—Pandits or strangers—leaving from or returning to the valley. For the first time, he felt guilty for having left Kashmir, as if it was he who had breached an unwritten trust between him and the Muslims.

The journey ended before Prem Nath realized it. His heart started beating faster and he was the last to get up from his seat and get down from the bus. Dusk had fallen. The earth under his feet felt unreal, as if he were standing on cotton wool. His legs were unsteady. He bent down to touch the ground with his hands and trembled with joy like a son meeting his loving mother after a long time. He breathed deeply the fresh and cool air of Srinagar and decided to foot the distance to his home. He was carrying just one hand bag and home was only a couple of kilometers away.

Walking again on the beaten paths and looking at the familiar buildings in Lal Chowk gave him a strange sense of oneness with his surroundings. While crossing the Amira Kadal Bridge, he looked into the serpentine river and smiled as he had not done for months. Suddenly, he realized that he had never really looked at the river all the busy years of his life, never taken in the details of the city, even the market where he ran his business, but taken it all for granted like one's own palm. How foolish of him to have left all this and how fortunate that he was back here.

As he neared home Prem Nath became nervous. His tread slowed and his heart started palpitating. It was already getting dark. Where would he go to spend the night if he found the house gutted or if someone had forcibly occupied it? For the first time since he left Jammu in the morning he rued his decision. The thirty minute walk seemed like an eternity. But at the bend of the road in his mohalla, he recognized his house from a distance and heaved a big sigh of relief. He quickened his step and almost ran the last hundred yards to catch his breath at his door. He touched it gently with trembling hands, quietly opened the padlock and found himself in his loving front yard. It was incredible to be back. He rushed inside to find everything as he had left it, as he walked from one room to another. He felt exhilarated. He dusted and kissed the idols and pictures of his deities on the mantelpiece, washed his face, and crept into his bed after eating the dinner his wife had packed for him in the morning. He could not believe it; to be back in his cozy home as if he had never left.

Prem Nath woke up early next morning. What a great feeling to be home, to have water running in the taps at all hours, to have your own bed and your own space, to tread the soft earth, to look at the plants, and hear the birds twitter in your own lawn. The grass had grown wild but it was so green, so soothing to the eyes after the stinging glare of the burning sun that ricocheted from the stray stones scattered around the Muthi Migrant Camp. He enjoyed a hearty bath he had missed all these months as he washed the grime and slime of exile with the purifying water of Kashmir. He drank a full glass; it tasted like nectar. He picked flowers from the shrubs and went out to visit the temple that was only a few hundred yards away from his home.

It was unusually quiet in the temple. There was a lone visitor—a woman sitting cross-legged in a corner of the prayer hall. Prem Nath recognized her immediately—his neighbour, Ambravati. They exchanged silent greetings. A strange fervour seized him. He washed the Siva lingam with water and anointed it with a pinch of saffron that he poured out from a tiny box secured in the inner pocket of his vest. He painted an oval blob of saffron tilak in the middle of his own forehead after a fleeting mental debate whether it would be safe to do so, for it would mark him out as a Pandit. In any case, Pandits and Muslims gave themselves away easily by their demeanor, dress and dialogue and he would not forgo the religious symbol that he had worn all his life even if it cost him his life. After all, he was returning not as a convert but a firm votary of his faith, and if he had to live in Kashmir he would do so as a proud Pandit. He offered flowers, burnt incense, chanted mantras and completed the puja.

Then, he sat in front of the lingam in contemplation. Howsoever he tried, he could not concentrate. Soon he started crying and burst into loud protestations: Lord, I have been a family man to the core—faithful, religious, and upright in my business. I worshipped you all my life, fasted on auspicious days, gave away in charity what I could afford. Why have you spurned me? What sins have I committed? Answer me, my lord; show me the light; give me strength to ride through this crisis.

Tears streamed down Prem Nath's eyes and he felt lighter after that catharsis of sorts. Courage filled him. He walked round the temple seven times and made an exit.

Ambravati was waiting for him in the temple porch. They exchanged greetings.

"When did you return?" she asked

"Last night."

"Are you staying on? How is Janki Bhabi? How are your children?" She spoke in whispers, glancing furtively around her, as if afraid to be caught speaking with him.

"Jammu is hell; I could not stand it any longer. I will give it a try here and, if all goes well, call back Janki and children. How is Kashi Nath?"

"He is fine as can be under the circumstances." She replied. "Do you intend to start working again?"

"Yes. In fact, I am looking forward to it eagerly."

"Why are you in such a hurry? You have just arrived. Take it easy. Take your time to settle down. See if you can adjust to life again in these changed circumstances. Resume your work only if you convince yourself that it will be safe to do so."

"I cannot wait another day. I am so eager to see my shop and to find out if all is well there." He heaved a deep sigh and asked, "The temple seems abandoned; are there no Pandits left in the neighborhood?"

"Almost every one has left except my husband and me. He cannot tolerate the heat and is afraid to face the prospect of summer in the plains. But things are getting worse here. There seems no end to the anarchy. We sent our son and his family away last month. They are worried about us and want us to join them. Let us see how long we can endure it here." She lowered her voice even further, "Please keep a low profile and be watchful; you can't trust anyone these days. Take care. May the lord protect you!"

With those words, she hurried home and Prem Nath walked to the family grocer to replenish his pantry. He would have breakfast before he set out to start work.

"So you have returned. You did not like it there, Prem Nath?" The grocer asked without showing much surprise on seeing him.

"Not really," Prem Nath replied. He had made it a point not to give any elaborate explanations.

"Are you going to stay or leave again?" the vendor went on.

"I had gone away temporarily for a breather; I hope I do not have to leave again."

"What about your family? Will they join you?"

"Of course they will."

"Inshallah," the grocer exclaimed

"Inshallah," echoed Prem Nath.

He had feared taunts and humiliation, but the exchange with the grocer passed off well, beyond his expectations. The invocation to Allah by the grocer elevated his spirits. He felt unusually happy and light footed and trotted home with the groceries.

***

On her return home from the temple, Ambravati went straight to her bed room. Kashi Nath, her husband, was waiting for her in the parlour. She did not exchange the usual pleasantries with him, nor did she go inside the kitchen to get breakfast ready as was her routine. This was quite odd. He followed her and found her lost in thought.

"Why do you look out of sorts?" Kashi Nath enquired.

"I am fine," she said looking out of the window.

"Something seems to be the matter," he persisted.

Kashi Nath hardly ever moved out of his house. Times were bad and anything was possible on the streets or in the marketplace. But he had failed to dissuade his wife from visiting the temple. It was a routine that she was used to from her childhood. She would not break it at any cost. In the thirty three years of their wedded life he had never come in the way of her other elaborate religious rituals—the observance of ashtamis, amavasyas, pooranmashis, and other important events. They were a part of her persona. Without them he would not recognize her. She would always return from the temple with a sense of fulfillment, her face flushed, and a sparkle in her eyes. But it was different today.

"There is nothing the matter," she replied, wringing her hands, avoiding his eyes.

"Did you meet any one on the way? Did anyone offend or threaten you? Why don't you tell me?" He was getting impatient.

"Not really. I saw Prem Nath at the temple," she replied, looking directly at him.

He could not immediately recall the name.

"Pray, which Prem Nath are you speaking about?"

"Why, have you forgotten Prem Nath, our neighbour? He has returned from Jammu."

Kashi Nath heaved a sigh of relief. "Well, that is good news.

When did he arrive? Has the whole family returned? Why should his return disturb you?"

"Because I have a strange premonition." She said in earnest.

"Come on, this is only a sign of the times we live in. Fear is lurking in every corner and we imagine horrible things. Now let us have some breakfast and tell me what happened at the temple."

She remained seated on her bed and resumed, "I watched Prem Nath inside the temple. After prayers he sat down in front of the lingam, started some kind of conversation with the lord, cried like a child and complained aloud to him. It was quite a sight. I could not concentrate on my meditation. I had visions of him being stalked. I have this strange foreboding of some harm coming to him. He told me he was going to open his shop today. I hope he stays safe."

Her husband was delighted to learn about Prem Nath's return from exile and described it an act of great courage. He wished more Pandits would return. It would give him reason to stay on. He dismissed her fears and decided to visit Prem Nath in the evening.

"We will go and see him," he declared.

Ambravati was sceptical. Visiting a returnee was considered an act of defiance by the militants who denounced the runaways as betrayers of Azadi, and decreed severe punishment for them and for those who showed any sympathy towards them. She feared the neighbours would find out and report it if they went to see Prem Nath.

"We will visit him quietly after sunset. The neighbourhood is almost deserted by then. No one will notice us. Don't you think he deserves our moral support at this crucial juncture?" said Kashi Nath.

"I do, yet, what of the apparition?" she asked

"Pray, what apparition are you speaking about?"

"When Prem Nath stepped inside the temple, I had finished my puja and was seated in the corner for my meditation. I tried hard but it was difficult to concentrate. My thoughts ran wild, my heart sank and my body quivered. As soon as I shut my eyes to meditate, I had strange visions—of a melee, of people going berserk, of frightening noises, of calls for help. Then I saw an apparition—a young bearded man in a *pheron*, with a skull cap and a gun. He is so vivid in my memory that I could spot him if he were real. I was horrified and wanted to run away from the temple. But I waited for Prem Nath until he came out. I wanted to warn him but stopped short and just asked him to be careful. My heart races even now as I relate this to you."

"Come on; put your thoughts in order. I know it has been hard on you with no one left here except the two of us. We will have to get over these obsessions with militancy and murder. We will visit Prem Nath in the evening and welcome him back. We must make him feel that he is not alone."

"I don't think it is safe to visit him. It is safe neither for us nor for him," she bared her fears again.

***

After breakfast, Prem Nath walked to his shop at Amira Kadal. More police bunkers were in evidence than when he had left, but the city was bustling with activity as usual. He could not spot a single Pandit among the pedestrians, and yet there was no evidence of the turmoil underneath the sheen of a crisp summer morning in Srinagar. The river, with low water levels at this time of the year, flowed ever so calm, the banks wide and bare. He looked in front of him and the Shankaracharya hill with the sun shining bright upon it stood in royal splendour.

He wondered why had he never really seen it before? The azure blue sky was a soulful contrast to the dull canopy of the Jammu sky in summer; the languorous clouds clung to the mountain cliffs in a passionate embrace. He saw all this as if it were for the first time in his life. He realized again that he had taken it all for granted and never really spent a thought on it. He promised to himself that he would not waste a moment of this bliss any more, now that he had returned. He smiled and felt a strange lightness of spirit, a bounce in his tread, a heightened sense of expectation.

Prem Nath spotted his shop from a distance and his heart took a leap. It was early for business. Hands trembling with nervous expectation, he opened the padlocks and raised the shutters to the familiar grating sound. He found everything as he had left it; nothing had been touched. He swept and dusted his shop, rearranged the cloth rolls, cleared the cobwebs, cleaned the couches and, making himself comfortable on his cushioned seat, looked around. Soon other shopkeepers started arriving and opening their shops.

Abdul Rahim, the proprietor of the shop directly across the street, saw him and shouted, "Look who is here!" And coming over, he addressed him with offended dignity, "So you are back, Prem Nath! Well, you did not even inform us when you left. And here you are again, and we have no knowledge when you arrived and why."

"Do you think I would want to leave my home willingly? It was at the insistence of my family. But I realized my mistake when I had to suffer the indignities and travails of exile. Well, my friend, I am sorry, but you know sometimes it is not within one's power. This was a mass exodus; I was not alone." Prem Nath spoke his heart.

"Did we not warn you against running away? But it seems

Governor Jagmohan had the last word and prevailed upon you Pandits to leave."

"To be honest, I had no such information. I fled because of the insecurity and the violence and mostly because of what happened in January. The decision was entirely my own. Nobody told me to leave. I had no intention of being gone for ever. But I am back now, happy to be with you all, safe in your company I suppose."

Prem Nath's genial statement eased the tension. An exchange of pleasantries followed. They inquired about each other's health, about their families and about business. There was even a belated hug. Prem Nath was pleased to learn that people in the market missed him and that some customers were asking about his whereabouts.

"We too are going through rough times, facing bullets from both sides—the militants and the army—but we will not spurn our mother Kashmir like you did. Azadi is for everyone, as much for you as for us. We have to face the consequences together, don't we?" Abdul Rahim opined forcefully.

Prem Nath nodded in agreement. On the whole, these words from his neighbour sounded reassuring and there was no point in contesting his statement about Azadi. He had rehearsed this encounter so many times in his mind. It did not pass off badly, he thought. He felt relaxed and invited Abdul Rahim for a cup of tea.

"I must be going now, we will meet later, Inshallah," Abdul Rahim excused himself.

But he was not gone long when he reappeared, accompanied by a burqa-clad figure.

"This is my cousin. Can she wait here in your shop till I return? I have to go on an errand; I will open my shop later. I won't be long."

And he was gone. The burqa-clad person sat on the couch.

Prem Nath began relating the experiences of Jammu to the veiled figure, addressing her as sister. She nodded but did not speak. He offered her tea. She declined, moving her head sideways. She was in the traditional burqa that covered the whole body and the face except for small openings in front of the eyes.

In about twenty minutes, two bearded young men, one wearing a *pheron* and a skull cap and the other in trousers and jacket, walked in. Prem Nath was excited to receive customers after a long break.

"What can I show you, Jenab?" he asked in utter humility.

"Well, we are looking for decent fabric for a Khan dress, something that is tough and will last," said the one in the *pheron*.

The veiled figure rose and walked quietly out of the shop. Prem Nath started picking rolls of cloth within his arm's reach and unfurling them for the two customers to see. They seemed fidgety, not really certain what they wanted, looking at the cloth rather cursorily. He pulled out some more rolls and opened them, commenting on the texture and the colour, the toughness of the fabric and the reasonable price. They wanted something different. He rose from his seat to bring down a roll from the upper shelves. As he turned to face them, the skullcap rose from the couch, produced a gun in a flash from under his *pheron*, and, pointing it at him, started hurling invectives:

"How dare you return here to rob others of their business? Have you not learnt your lesson yet, Panditji? We have no need here for you and your ilk—usurers, informers and deserters."

Prem Nath was wild-eyed and speechless with terror.

The skullcap fired a shot.

Prem Nath fell down on his outstretched hands. The cloth roll hit the assailant, and his gun flew to the floor. Prem Nath screamed aloud, calling for help. The young men picked up the gun hurriedly and vanished. By the time Prem Nath collected himself, people had started pouring in. The bullet had pierced his chest on the left side. He was bleeding. The crowd hailed a three-wheeler taxi to take him to the civil hospital.

Prem Nath refused any help. He did not want a three-wheeler nor would he go to the civil hospital. How could he trust anyone now? He had heard of militants following their victims to the hospital to complete the unfinished task if they survived the attack. Meanwile, a couple of BSF police constables arrived on the scene. His spirits revived, but he was fainting from the loss of blood.

"Please take me to the military hospital in the cantonment. Please take me in a police van, otherwise they will certainly kill me," Prem Nath pleaded and fell unconscious.

***

Ambravati felt uneasy the whole afternoon. Her morning visions kept coming back to her. To dispel the disturbing thoughts and fears she busied herself with chores that had remained undone for long. Though she had dissuaded her husband from visiting Prem Nath for fear of reprisals from the militants, she now wished they had visited him and made sure he was safe. Her husband too did not bring up the subject that was uppermost in his thoughts. They sat for dinner and just when they turned the radio on there was a news flash: A migrant Pandit was shot at by two unidentified assailants in his shop at Amira Kadal. He was shifted immediately to the Cantonment Hospital where his condition is reported to be critical.

Ambravati and Kashi Nath spent the longest night of their lives in fear and panic. Far from visiting Prem Nath, they collected the most meager of their possessions and left the house quietly in the morning to take the first bus to Jammu.

Prem Nath battled for his life in the hospital.

6
SALIGRAM'S SECRET

I came to know Saligram Bhat when he brought his mother to my outpatients in the early seventies. She had stones in her gall bladder that gave her severe colic and cried for removal. A surgeon who had been consulted kept postponing surgery on one pretext or the other. Possibly, he did not feel confident about the outcome in view of her old age and frail health. Saligram would not give up. He kept insisting. The surgeon sent her to me for medical clearance.

I wrote back to the surgeon that he could go ahead with the operation. But he remained sceptical and counselled the patient that it was better for her to suffer an occasional bout of colic, which could always be managed, than submit to a risky surgical procedure.

Saligram lived with his widowed mother in a small house at Chattabal in downtown Srinagar. He was a lowly employee in the Food and Supplies Department that handled the acquisition and distribution of food grains. If his mother died, he would be orphaned and condemned to a lonely life. He was disconsolate and did not know whom to turn to. He sought my opinion again.

I was rather disappointed with the surgeon. Here was a simple case of gall stones; why did he refuse surgery unless he had an arcane hunch that she would die on the table? Had Saligram's bearing put him off?

Saligram was thin and short, hardly five feet, and one eyed, having lost the other eye early in childhood in an accident. He wore a glass eye that looked squarely and rather inquiringly at you. His nose which had taken after his mother's—flat with flared nostrils—was rather large for his small face. His lips were thick and his cheeks hollow, and he wore a pencil-moustache which was never trimmed properly. But, of all things, it was the faux karakuli he wore on his head that lent him an eerie look—random strands of discoloured hair showing from below the cap. The fur on the karakuli had worn off in irregular patches like his hair. He never took his cap off even in summer when sweat trickled down his face. It was the same cap he wore day in and day out. Perched on his snub nose, he wore thick lenses in a heavy, horn-rimmed frame, that completed the rather comic appearance of this innocuous man.

It was his very oddity that drew me to him. Beneath his rather strange exterior, I found an intelligent, perceptive man who was unhappy. I wanted to help him in whatever way I could to alleviate his anxiety.

I spoke with another surgeon. She was new in the faculty, struggling for recognition, and waiting for an opportunity to prove herself. Here was the chance—a patient whom a senior surgeon had turned down.

Not surprisingly, surgery turned out to be a tame affair. The gall bladder filled with stones was removed and shown to the waiting son outside the operation theatre. The gallstones were given to him. He looked at them with awe, even reverence, folded them neatly in a handkerchief and pocketed them as a memento. Tears ran down his healthy eye; the glass eye glistened with gratitude.

Ever since Saligram was beholden to me for, what he deemed, a gesture of kindness on my part. He became my fan and brought his mother regularly for a check up in my clinic. He often visited my home after his office hours, ingratiating himself with my family, in due course to become a regular hanger-on. He would wash my car on Sundays, do odd jobs when our domestic help was busy with other chores, sit and gossip with my mother and confide in her everything about his rather lonesome life—his hopes and fears, his disappointment with his brothers, his devotion to his mother and her sacrifices for the family.

Kakni, as he called his mother affectionately, had lost her husband early. He had left her with three sons and a daughter. She had married off the daughter, Prabha, soon after. Her older son, Jagan Nath, was employed as a ward officer in the municipality, a lowly position in the social hierarchy. He parted from the joint household after he took a wife. The youngest son, Omkar, was the only one in the family to graduate from college. He stumbled on a gazetted job and this went immediately to his head. From what he considered his elevated position, he felt it beneath his status to mingle or identify with his brothers. Since he was posted at Jammu, he lost touch with his family and hardly ever visited Kashmir.

Saligram was a peon. His job was to carry office files from one table to another, from the lower division clerk to the higher division clerk and from there to the deputy superintendent, the superintendent, the accountant, the deputy director and the director, all the way up the office hierarchy. He sat on a stool outside the main office hall and waited for the bell to ring when he would rush inside and carry out the orders of his superiors. His appearance often made him the butt of jokes. He bore the insults quietly even as he witnessed the murky goings-on in the department that was notorious for pilferage of food grains and funds. When his spirits sank low, he came to our house to seek solace. My father would, in his characteristic style and humour, ask him to relate the *khabre Zainakadal*—the rumours that emanated from offices and busy shopping squares like Zainakadal. He would often suggest, jokingly, that he get married before it was too late. After all, his mother would not last for ever.

The subject of marriage was dear to Saligram's heart. It was his unfulfilled wish to remarry by any means, if only to prove to the world that the fiasco of his first marriage was an aberration; that the bride had run away because she had an affair with another man and not because of his looks. Yet, it was not easy to acquire a wife. His mother had failed and no one else was bothered to see him settled in blissful wedlock, not even his sister who had maintained regular contact with the family after she had married. She feared that her mother Kakni would lose the only caregiver, if he married and set up a separate household.

It was during one of those intimate conversations with father that Saligram finally laid bare his pining heart. He bashfully asked if there was anyone who could help find a wife for him from Kishtwar. He had heard that Kishtwar was the last hope for bachelors, widowers or divorcees.

Kishtwar, situated at about five thousand feet, is one of the most backward areas in Jammu and Kashmir. There are numerous hamlets in this remote region, locked away in mountainous ranges with access through dense forests, there being no roads and no electricity. Poverty and penury is rife, disease and death haunt many families, and orphans and widows abound. Many are landless peasants; those with land cannot grow enough to last them the whole year. Young boys migrate to Srinagar or Jammu, the twin capitals of Jammu and Kashmir, in search of a living. They end up as helping hands to bakers and cooks, or as domestic servants.

City men of all denominations—unmarried men who are unable to find mates for one reason or the other, widowers, divorcees and others—are often found levitating to these forbidding heights to find a match. The match makers make merry and often come up with a solution to the most vexed cases. Kishtwar is the final refuge of many hopeless matrimonial candidates and she disappoints only the most unfortunate.

Saligram wanted to try his luck in the marketplace of Kishtwar.

We did not have to seek far. Cousin Makhan Lal Dhar was the natural choice to go to, as a go between. Posted at Kishtwar as an agricultural officer, he was quite familiar with the terrain and the denizens. He had met Saligram at our place on several occasions and was favourably disposed towards him. However, he conveyed at the very outset, that Saligram should not expect a virgin, given his status, age and physicality. A widow was the best bet, he declared. Saligram agreed but haggled for a widow without any dependant children. Only in an untenable situation would he settle for a widow with just one child. Times were difficult and it was not easy to take care of a large family. Saligram's father had, however, left him some ancestral farmland in Zainakoot which he had converted into an apple orchard. For the last couple of years the small landholding had yielded a modest harvest to augment his income.

Unfortunately for Saligram, the marriage market in Kishtwar was passing through a difficult time. There was a scarcity of childless widows. Even widows with one or two children had been snitched away by eager bidders with better qualifications. Cousin Makhan Lal finally communicated that there was a likely candidate—a poor widow with three kids. I called Saligram and explained the situation. It was depressing news. The prospect of a large brood and a cackling mother hen disturbing the quiet of his home gave him the creeps. He did not know how to address the proposal. But the desire for a wife proved greater than the pain of a large family the bride would bring with her. He discussed it with his mother. She was a simple woman, contented with her life. But she wanted to see him settled. This was her last wish. She gave it some thought and advised her son to take the plunge.

We informed Makhan Lal of the decision and asked him to go ahead. Word came soon after, that a meeting had been arranged and Saligram should be dispatched to Kishtwar. We advised the prospective groom to put on his best clothes, keep his chin up, change his glasses to fit the bridge of his nose, and to replace his *karakuli* with a Gandhi cap that might suit him better. But he would not part with his *karakuli*. It was as if it were a part of his anatomy. It was like asking him to leave his head behind.

Armed with papers testifying to his status as a peon in the Food and Supplies Department, and the revenue record of the orchard that brought added income, a gold ring and a shawl (which my mother had asked him to carry as a gift for his would-be bride if an agreement came about), Saligram set off in a bus for Kishtwar, his mind in turmoil at the grim prospect of having to take care of three kids and an unknown widow from the land of the witches. Yes, many believed that women from Kishtwar worked witchcraft on their husbands to keep them from fooling around. If a man betrayed or abandoned his wife, she would follow him in the guise of a hawk wherever he went and, unbeknownst to him, nibble away at his heart and his liver till he died a terrible death.

Makhan Lal gave him a warm welcome. Next day, his meeting was arranged with the widow's brother who had some questions to ask this gentleman who would marry his sister and take in her children. When the time came, he was taken aback by Saligram's appearance and bearing, notwithstanding the brand new outfit that he was wearing. Makhan Lal was present during the meeting and made a strong case for the prospective groom, advancing the documents as proof of his financial stability. Saligram was like a student under the scrutiny of an inspector of schools; but a student too old for his grade! He had streaks of grey already showing at the temples, deep creases that furrowed his face, and a slight hunch from stooping to his officers—all of which made him look older than his forty-five years. He felt wretched and wanted to call off the interview. But the unfulfilled wish for a wife got the better of him and he kept quiet, like a lamb ready to go under the knife. It was after a lot of debate that the brother agreed to take the proposal forward. There was a last formality, though. The widow and Saligram must meet.

Was it the stars that were unfavorably placed, or was it the poor light of the lantern that made him look pale and dismal? When Saligram was ushered into the room where the widow was waiting to receive him, she uttered a loud shriek and swooned, as if she had seen a ghost. Saligram shrank back, sweating profusely, shaking with fright. Makhan Lal and the widow's brother moved forward to revive her. They fanned the widow's brow, rubbed her soles and opened her clenched jaws to make her drink some water. As soon as she recovered she asked them about the apparition, now slumped in a corner.

"That is the bridegroom," her brother explained.

"Under no circumstances will I marry that frightful creature, even if he be the Prince of Kashmir," she protested.

No amount of persuasion would bring her round. It was unfortunate for Saligram that she turned out to be a pretty woman. It was a total mismatch. He had offered the last sacrifice but it was no use. He returned home, downhearted and empty handed and never talked of marriage after that incident.

Saligram continued with his life—uneventful and unchanging from one day to another. His looks aside, he had a serious failing— he was an inveterate miser. He spent very little and hardly ever participated in social events. He never went to a picnic or a movie. Ever since I knew him he wore the same jacket, the same *pheron* and, of course, the same *karakuli* from one year to the next. He had no bad habits, never smoked, never chewed a betel leaf, and never snuffed a substance. Possibly, he had been saving for the eventuality of having to pay dowry for a bride, if ever one came his way. That seemed a remote possibility now, even though he might not have put the thought away for good. The only event he celebrated was his birthday when he invited me to his home for lunch. His mother cooked fish, kalia and lotus root. There would be no other guests except, sometimes, his sister Prabha. She was the only relative who visited them, and Saligram showered lots of affection on her. She shared their sorrows and joys, and lent a feminine touch to the home of an aged woman and a chronic bachelor. It was a humble cottage—two rooms, and a kitchen—enough for mother and son. I often wondered where he would have accommodated the widow and her brood had his marriage materialized. There was peace and harmony here, and love in abundance. The mother adored her one-eyed darling, and he in return lavished all his devotion on her. Perhaps the Kishtwar fiasco was providential. Saligram would have been crushed under the weight of an unmanageable family. His mother might not have retained her peace for long though she wanted so much to see her son settled.

***

Come 1989 and Kashmir was in flames. There was terror in the air, terror in every heart, terror in homes that had been havens of peace and security. It struck all—the young and old, men and women, the high and the low. Pandits started fleeing their homes and hearths to the unknown terrains of exile, since they were the main targets of terrorists. Saligram bided his time even as his Pandit neighbours were leaving in droves. He was loath to leave. Where would he go with his old mother? Would she survive in the hot climate of Jammu where most of the Pandits were seeking refuge? His Food and Supplies Department was getting depleted of Pandit employees even as he watched in dismay. His Muslim colleagues eyed him suspiciously, taunting him for staying back when others had fled. It was the same story in his neighbourhood. The milkmaid, the grocer, the vegetable seller, the butcher and the passers by looked suspiciously at him as if he were an alien.

The decision to leave was painful. His mother hoped her other son Omkar, who was stationed in Jammu, would welcome them to his house, even though he had never visited them after he left Kashmir nearly a decade earlier. They did not have his address but they would find out from his office once they reached Jammu.

It was the middle of April 1990. The bus arrived late in the evening. By that time the offices had closed. Jammu was already blazing hot. A group of volunteers from Sahitya Samiti, a relief organization set up by the Hindu community in Jammu, were waiting at the bus stand, receiving refugees. They put them up in various temples, ashrams, and dharamsalas. The old and the sick had priority for placement. Saligram and mother were lucky to be provided just body space in the huge hall of the Kashmiri Pandit Sabha at Ambphalla which was already overflowing with refugees. There was a chaotic scramble for space and services—just a single kitchen, bathroom and lavatory for scores of refugees. People were huddled inside the hall, children fighting and shrieking, old people groaning, young men and women arguing.

It was a nightmare for every one in that hall. Next morning, Saligram set out to meet his brother in his office. He was new to Jammu but made it to the destination, inquiring from shopkeepers and pedestrians on the way.

When Omkar was informed about a visitor from Kashmir, he came out of his office and saw his brother in the corridor. They were meeting after a decade.

"Namaskar," Saligram greeted his brother.

Omkar turned stiff, nodding his head in greeting without speaking.

"We reached here late last evening and had to stay in a hall for the night. It is cramped with refugees. Kakni is dying to see you," Saligram said with humility.

"I am sorry, but if you came here to seek shelter, you have come to the wrong place," Omkar retorted pokerfaced.

"We are literally on the street. You need not worry about me, but can you take in Kakni for a few days till I find suitable accommodation? She is in great distress and I am afraid she might die before the next sunrise." Saligram pleaded.

"There are thousands that have streamed out from Kashmir. The Relief Department is providing tents for them and I advise you to claim one for yourself and mother before they run out of supplies. She has always been comfortable with you. You need to stay together. I have earned with painstaking effort, some standing in the office and in the society here. Please do not tarnish it by announcing that you are my brother." The younger brother—curt, offensive, insulting— retreated inside.

Saligram was downcast. He did not know that his own brother would treat him like a pariah. It would hurt his mother to know she had been spurned by her son. He lied to her that he could not find Omkar's address and would try again another day.

After many trying months and numerous visits to the Relief Commissioner's office, mother and son were allotted a tent in Mishriwalla Migrant Camp where they settled down and adopted a routine as if they had always lived there. It is amazing how humans adjust to change, how they bear pain and suffer deprivation, how the body acclimatizes and the mind reconciles.

Saligram's mother did not die as he had feared, not for a long time. She carried on with her son, cooking for him and washing clothes at the community tap, while he went about the numerous formalities of registration as a refugee. Being an employee, he was not entitled to Rs. 450 that was affixed by the government as monthly dole for each refugee, nor was his mother. It took several months to get his bank account transferred to Jammu. There was a mad rush for these transfers. The bank managers were overwhelmed with work and found it expedient to ignore him with his odd looks and bearing.

Saligram found me within days of my arrival in Jammu, an exile like the rest of the Pandits. I was astonished to see him, and it took me several minutes to recognize him, for something that defined him was missing. Here he was—the same short and slender figure, the same horn-rimmed thick glasses, the same shirt and waistcoat, the same glass eye. What was different? Oh yes, the *karakuli*, that permanent fixture on his head, was missing. He looked dwarfish but dignified, even likable, with the stray hair combed carefully back in an unsuccessful attempt to hide the bald patches, the pitted scars, and the salt-and-pepper pigmentation. Having resisted parting with that faithful companion all his life, the searing heat of Jammu summer had succeeded where human endeavor had failed. Terrorism deprived him of his home and hearth, exile separated him from his *karakuli*.

"Do my eyes deceive me? You really are Saligram, aren't you? Where have you left your *karakuli*?" I asked him as he rushed into my arms, his frail body quivering in my embrace, his head just reaching my chin.

"The wild wind of Jihad blew it away!" Saligram had not lost his sense of humour.

It took me some time to reconcile to this man without his cap and to adjust to his changed demeanor—the migrant demeanor. For, displacement brought a unique change in peoples' bearing, their attitudes and thinking, their dress and demeanor, even the idiom and expression. There he was again—my devotee, my hanger on, my Hanuman. Yes, the devotee Hanuman and his lord Rama as my mother would often characterize the two of us. And, he resumed his visits to my place with greater frequency, now that he had no home and no office to go to.

Over the years Saligram grew remote and melancholy. He found himself utterly lost. He could not strike new friendships with the refugee campers who were mostly from the villages and treated city-bred folk with traditional suspicion, even hostility. They looked at him in disdain in spite of his friendly overtures. His sister Prabha came to see him now and then. She too had moved out of Kashmir—her husband, a police constable, having been transferred to Jammu and allotted a small apartment in the police quarters. Jagan Nath, the older brother, also visited them once in a while. He was one of the several Pandits who had purchased small plots of land some years earlier, having foreseen the tragic eventuality of exile. It had been a thoughtful investment. He built a couple of rooms for his family and moved out of the tent that was allotted to him. He expressed regret that he could not take his mother in for want of space.

Kakni felt even lonelier when Saligram sulked away in a corner of the tent. She worried about him as if he were a child, and wished more than ever that he were settled in family life. But that was a wish that she would take with her to the other world. Yes, Kakni was dying. Five terrible summers in a tent had drained her of her energy, stiffened her joints, bent her back, singed her grey hair, and stolen her appetite. Finally, she lost the will to live. All she desired was to return to Kashmir, to die there, and her ashes to be immersed in the sacred waters at Shadipur where the Vitasta meets the Sindh. There, her soul would find eternal solace.

But that was not to be. When Jagan Nath sensed that she was in the last lap of her mortal journey, he asked his brother and mother to move into his house. By then, he had built an additional room on the first floor and it would suffice for the two, he explained. It was a hard decision for Kakni, having grown accustomed to living with Saligram all the time. Moving at this stage would deprive them of the independence and the freedom of living in a tent where there were no amenities but also no restraints, that go with living in someone's house, even your son's. It was a strange peace that they had found in the tent at Mishriwalla Migrant Camp. The famous Kashmiri maxim, 'Nangas nender prangas peth'—one with no belongings sleeps soundly on bare floor—was so apt in their situation.

But, coming from her elder son, she did not have the heart to reject the offer. The chains of blood are stronger than steel and do not snap easily, she said when she finally moved. She wished now more than ever to see Omkar. She hoped the prodigal son would return one day.

Alas, that happened only after she breathed her last. Omkar did turn up for the cremation. All the siblings participated in the funeral rites. Jagan Nath, the older son, took the lead role in the rituals. Saligram would have liked to take this role because of his lifelong association with his mother but he was stricken with grief. The last words of his mother rang loud in his ears. "How will you face the world alone after I am gone? It is never late in life to find a companion for oneself," she had said in her dying moments.

Saligram did not see me for several months. He became morose and detached, for he lost the purpose and the meaning of life which had revolved around his mother. Nor could he find the privacy he so much desired now, if only to take stock of his life. He rued the decision to give up his tent which had now been allotted to another refugee. However, he found a new preoccupation. Within two months of his mother's demise, his retirement became due. He was now moving from one office to an other to get his pension order issued, to secure his gratuity and other benefits of superannuation.

It was during this time that his health showed signs of decline. He developed a loss of appetite and a feeling of fullness after meals. He wished the problem away while he was pursuing the settlement of his pension through the official bureaucracy, and deferred seeing me till he got his claim settled. By then, he was hardly able to eat more than a morsel without feeling bloated and wanting to throw up. He was getting weaker by the day. That is when he came to see me.

His wan face, bent frame and loss of weight were shocking. He looked like a ghost, like someone who had just risen from the grave.

"I have been urging him to see you but he never bothered. Please do something for him, doctor." Jagan Nath, who accompanied him, seemed genuinely concerned.

I got the tests done. There was a suspicion of malignancy of the stomach. A biopsy confirmed it. I wrote a referral to a surgical colleague.

There was no news from Saligram for a long time. I was under the impression that he was recuperating from surgery and possibly undergoing chemotherapy. When I sent for him, it was Jagan Nath who came to inform me that he had left for Delhi along with Omkar. I was surprised. This was the first time Saligram had ignored my advice. Why did he decide to go elsewhere for treatment when it was available for free in Jammu? Had he lost faith in me from a sense of disillusionment that many exiles suffered with friends and well-wishers? Or had he rediscovered his younger brother who had spurned him all his life. 'Blood bonds do not easily break,' his mother had said.

Jagan Nath informed me that Omkar, in an over-solicitous concern for his brother, had prevailed upon him to seek a second opinion in Delhi. He had posed several questions to his ailing brother: What had Jammu to offer in terms of medical treatment? Life was more precious than all the wealth in the world. What was he saving for all his life if not for his own well being? Did he not wish to live long? What had he seen of life to date, spending all of it serving his superiors and caring for his mother? Many fellow refugees had built their own houses, what about him? Could he not sell off the house in Chattabal back home in Kashmir and get in touch with a broker for his orchard? And finally, marriage was still an option; had he not heard of Englishmen marrying in old age?

Omkar's sermons had had a magical effect. The renewed dreams of matrimony had kindled the silent embers that still burned deep in Saligram's heart. He had finally yielded to his brother's persuasions.

"I will soon leave for Delhi. After all he is my brother. Besides, I cannot leave him to the machinations of Omkar. Prabha has already left for Delhi to be by his side," Jagan Nath confided.

"Omkar is only doing his brother a good turn. He may have changed after Kakni's death and this is how he wants to make amends.

Your mother put great store by the golden bonds of kinship, did she not?" I tried to put his mind at ease.

"Omkar broke those bonds long back. He is an impostor. He knows, as we all do, that Saligram lived frugally and saved every penny he could all his life, besides coming into a tidy sum from his pension claim last month. There is his house in Kashmir and a small orchard too. That builds up to a small fortune. I am sure Omkar is up to mischief, to grab it all. I should not be speaking like this while he is still alive, but cancer does not spare any one."

"So you and your sister are going to Delhi to keep vigil not on your sick brother but on your share of his savings?" I asked in disgust.

He turned red with shame. "No sir, that is not so. God is my witness. I always cared a lot for my brother. Did I not build an extra room in my house to welcome him and mother as soon I had the means? Did I not perform all the religious rituals for my mother after her demise? Did I not persuade him to see you as soon as I realized he was unwell?"

"Yes, you have been quite considerate and kind to your brother," I replied, even as I felt that, having rejected him all his life, and in a bid to claim his inheritance, his siblings now vied with each other to be with him like vultures hovering over a wounded prey.

Saligram was in Delhi for three weeks. It was a difficult surgery complicated by hemorrhage. He never recovered and the doctors asked the family to take him to die in peace among his loved ones.

Alas, when Saligram breathed his last, a few days after his return to Jammu, there was no peace anywhere but the rumblings of discord amongst the loved ones who had travelled to Delhi to be by his side. They suspected each other of having wheedled him secretly into signing a will and handing over his house documents, land papers and bank details.

When I saw the corpse, it grinned at me from the unfazed glass eye that seemed to tell all. Having known Saligram intimately, I doubted very much if any of them had succeeded. His mother had told him that people were born again to realize the unfulfilled wishes of their present life. He was quite capable of saving whatever he had for his next life.

7
A PLACE TO DIE

Cancer is a horrific disease; terminal cancer is death waiting in the shadows. Waiting, yet in no hurry to pounce on its victim and gobble it up. It goes about its work with methods its own, like the wily cat that has caught a mouse in its paws, which it lets go only to catch it again, tantalizing and terrorizing, turning and twisting, throwing it up and dashing it down, enough to paralyze but not to kill at once. When the victim is prostrate and helpless, he begs for mercy and cries for release, which comes only when death is ready to embrace him.

Brij Nath Daftari, a sixty-two-year-old retired clerk in the Ordinance Department of the Central Government, was suffering from terminal pancreatic cancer. He had lived all his life in Sheetal Nath, a suburb of Srinagar densely populated with Kashmiri Pandits, and the hub of their social, cultural and religious activities. The place is not far from where I lived near the famous Ramji Temple.

I knew Brij Nath from the time he came to me with his little daughter Rita who had contracted tuberculosis. Subsequently I treated his son Ashok for a rheumatic affliction of the heart, and his wife for various ailments. I became their family physician and friend until the time the valley was overtaken by a cataclysm that bruised and sundered relationships and drove hundreds of thousands into exile.

Brij Nath landed in Jammu in the first wave of the exodus in the winter of 1989-90. He was one of the estimated three hundred and fifty thousand Pandits hounded out when terror and violence had Kashmir in a deathly grip. The exodus scattered the Pandits like people in a shipwreck. Some drowned in the first storm of violence, others found rafts that carried them to far off lands, yet others are still floating in the choppy seas and struggling to reach shores.

Within a few months of his arrival in Jammu, Brij Nath fell ill. The family had lost contact with most of their relatives and friends. They were alone and miserable and did not know where to turn for help. They looked for me but I was still in Srinagar. Much later, in May 1990, I moved to Delhi and spent eight trying months there before I landed in Jammu. By that time, he had been going from one doctor to another. Soon after I settled down in rented lodgings, word went round in the refugee camps, and patients started pouring in. Brij Nath's family located me eventually and brought him for treatment.

Brij Nath had never been ill ever since I knew him. He was always sparsely built, lean, and sallow complexioned. I could barely recognize him now. He was rundown and a shade darker, partly from exposure to the harsh sun of Jammu and partly from his affliction. He stooped with pain, his eyes bulged with fear and he looked a shadow of his old self—a distorted, dwarfed shadow. He wore an unmistakable cancer visage. By the time I heard his story and examined him, the visage grew more pronounced. The disease had spread. It was the beginning of the end.

Without much ado, I divulged the prognosis to his son. By then, he had exhausted all his physical and financial reserves and though the news that his father would not last long came as a shock, he could not hide a sense of relief. Now Ashok was free to organize the ritual of terminal care without having to run after doctors and subjecting his father to unending medical tests and procedures.

There was nothing to be done except to alleviate Brij Nath's pain and let him die in peace. But peace, like a complex mathematical equation, has so many variables. The logistics were formidable in this case. How could one arrange a peaceful end for someone living in exile and suffering from the grinding pain of terminal cancer with hardly a roof over his head, and no place to die?

When his relatives came to learn of his illness and his deteriorating condition, they started pouring in. Most of them were refugees, who like him, had fled Kashmir and had little else to do except to search for their lost relatives and friends and to share tales of the travails they had to go through—scouring for shelter and sustenance, finding schools for their children and hospitals for their sick, establishing new contacts, striking new roots. The least they could do was to visit each other and share their sorrow.

The landlord was unhappy when he figured out the number of people visiting his sick tenant everyday, from the piles of footwear outside the one room he had rented out to Brij Nath and his family—his wife, son and daughter. He did not like crowds in his already cramped house. The traffic in the shared corridor and the shared toilet was too much to bear. The place was getting choked. He threatened to evict the tenants if the traffic continued. But the family could not stop visitors. That was just not done. Kashmiri Pandits do not shut their doors to monks, mendicants or mongrels; there was no question of shutting it on relatives, friends and well-wishers. But the landlord saw no logic in this argument and asked them to quit. They offered to pay additional rent but he had made up his mind. He gave them a month's notice.

Ashok went from door to door to find a place but there was no space available anywhere. The family had found the present accommodation in Sarwal without any difficulty, having been amongst the early arrivals. Now, Jammu was bursting at the seams with the avalanche of refugees who settled down to inhabit any conceivable space available in houses, stables, cellars and stores. Rents hit the roof. The tents provided by the government were all taken. Some old and dilapidated buildings were thrown open to accommodate the rush. Those who found no place in Jammu moved to neighbouring towns—Samba, Kathua, Kishtwar, Doda, Kud, Batote. Many others filtered down to Punjab, Himachal and Haryana. A lot more moved to Delhi, and the rest to other metropolises. The refugees got rapidly scattered all over India as violence and mayhem escalated in the valley and the exodus from Kashmir gained momentum.

As the deadline to quit the Sarwal lodging got closer and his frustration mounted, Ashok met an old friend by chance, who knew of a family with a spare room. Together, they went to have a look. It was a poorly ventilated room in a dilapidated house in the innermost recesses of the old city, accessed through narrow lanes where pedestrians had to squeeze themselves to avoid brushing against each other. There was no choice, however. Ashok accepted the offer, hoping the family would somehow tide over this turbulent period of their lives in this bleak retreat.

That was a false hope, though. It was literally moving from the frying pan into the fire. Brij Nath's condition deteriorated rapidly. He grew claustrophobic in this dark damp room. The plaster was peeling off the walls, sculpting monstrous shapes that took the visage of Yama and frightened him. A small window in a wrought-iron frame looked out at the grimy lane outside, bringing in stench from the drains. He asked them to keep it shut but that made the room even hotter. The fan, the only means available to beat the heat, blew gusts of hot air on his already febrile and famished frame.

Were these the burning fires of hell that he had heard about? Was he really dying? How long did he have to go through this agony before the end came? Brij Nath's thoughts often wandered to his past. Back home, he had lived frugally right from his childhood, yet always in peace and contentment. His father had left him a modest dwelling and a small front yard with a solitary pomegranate tree and a small flowerbed where he planted marigolds for his gods. He offered these fresh when they bloomed, and dried the surplus for winter use. There was a rose bush near the porch that he doted upon like his own child. He had worked hard to provide education for his son and daughter. But there were unfinished responsibilities that plagued his troubled soul. Ashok, an agricultural graduate, was jobless. Rita, a commerce student, was without a trousseau and yet to be married off. What tortured him most was the thought of his wife, much younger than him, donning the mantle of widowhood. He wanted to go back to Kashmir and die there in his ancestral home. He repeated this wish every day to his family: "It is better to face the bullets in Kashmir than burn in the living hell here."

Painkillers did not work and Brij Nath groaned day and night as the pain grew worse. It came in fits and spasms, and his anguished cries tore the stillness of the night. It was not long before the landlord complained to the family: "For several days now, your patient has been howling all the time, rousing the whole neighbourhood. Pray, who is treating him?"

They replied that their patient was in the hands of their family physician and he was the best they knew. He was not impressed.

"I have not heard of this doctor you speak about. Why don't you go and get a local specialist? Your patient may be suffering from some regional affliction which your doctor is not familiar with. It will take the refugee doctors some time before they are acquainted with problems specific to this place. I would suggest you contact the famous Dr. Gandotra. He is the best in town."

Ashok had no choice but to keep his landlord in good humour. He found the doctor's address and brought him to see his father. The patient was not happy with a doctor he did not know and with whom he could neither communicate freely in his own language nor establish rapport. But he was asked to bear with this arrangement for some time. Dr. Gandotra ordered more tests and prescribed a different set of medicines.

Brij Nath was wasting away fast. Days and nights merged in a miasma of nausea and retching, escalating pain and exhaustion. His complexion took on an eerie hue of black and yellow. The landlord sensed the specter of death in the room. It made him uncomfortable as the spectre grew bigger every day, threatening to shroud his own dwelling. He did not like the idea of his tenant dying in his house.

He had learned of the elaborate Kashmiri Pandit rituals associated with dying and the post-funeral rites that extended beyond the days of mourning. There would be the tenth day ceremony when all the relatives and friends would gather at the riverbank to watch the son tonsure his head, take a bath, make rice balls to feed the departed, and immerse the ashes in the river. This would be followed by three days of more elaborate rites–the shraddhas and yajnas-with prayers to Agni, the god of fire. All these would draw large crowds. The fortnightly, monthly, and six-monthly ceremonies would surely perpetuate the traffic in and out of the house. No, he would not allow this in his house.

"Mr Ashok, your father is getting worse every day. You will have to do something about it," the landlord called him aside.

"I know. We have tried everything, including the doctor you recommended, and even the *phanda* that your wife suggested."

"But he is dying, can't you see?"

"Yes, he is deteriorating fast. My mother keeps hoping he will turn the corner but the doctors do not give much hope."

"You will have to leave my house before the time comes."

"That cannot be, sir. Where will we go with a dying man? You have been kind to rent us your room; please bear with us a little longer."

"I do not like a stranger dying in my house. It is a bad omen. You must move before it is too late."

"Please give me a few days and I will start looking for a room elsewhere," Ashok begged him.

The landlord was unmoved. "You must find another place right away, before you find your belongings on the street," he threatened.

Ashok was on the hunt once again for alternative lodgings. He sounded out his relatives and friends. He searched for a room in the immediate neighbourhood and in the distant suburbs but drew a blank. The landlord visited his father every evening, saw death closing in, and repeated his warning. Ashok avoided him as far as possible and returned home late, much after the landlord had gone to bed.

Brij Nath was sinking deeper into the twilight zone between light wakefulness and stupor. His son came rushing to me with a fervent plea: "Doctor, my father's condition is critical. He is fading away fast and the landlord wants us to quit before he dies. Please do something, try some miracle drug to keep him alive a little longer till I find a place for him to die. Please doctor, could you try some medications that we have not tried so far, that might give him a little relief."

It was heart wrenching. I had watched this young man grow from a child, carrying the burden of an enlarged heart condition and a larger family responsibility. I did not know how to help him but an idea flashed in my mind.

"Why don't you place an ad in the local newspaper? There may be someone out there who has a room to spare."

"But we will have to keep quiet about father's illness. Will any one rent us a room with the knowledge that we will be moving in with a dying person?" Ashok asked.

"On the contrary, I feel you should be honest about it. You do not want to be thrown out yet again after you find a place," I said.

"I have no idea how to phrase the advertisement," he said timidly.

I scribbled on a piece of paper and handed it over to him. The advertisement appeared the next day in the local newspaper, with my contact number since Ashok did not own a phone.

Wanted: A Place to Die.

Family of four, one of them sick and dying, in desperate need of lodgings.

Size of accommodation and rent no consideration; just enough space to die.

When all seems lost, there is hope lurking somewhere in the least likely place, like a lotus blooming in a pool of mud.

Sardar Gurbax Singh of Nanak Nagar phoned me the same evening. He had two rooms to let; would I care to have a look? I sent for Ashok and directed him to the address. "Whatever the rent, go ahead and strike a deal," I urged him.

Gurbax Singh was a jovial Sikh, the kindness of his heart matching the span of his broad and bushy moustache that he twirled after every sentence he spoke. He invited Ashok for a cup of tea before he showed him two medium sized, well ventilated, lightly furnished rooms. Ashok could not believe his luck. The ideal place to live, he thought to himself, and to die.

He inquired about the rent.

"Who is bothered about the rent, young man? Pay whatever you think is right and when you have the money. I demand no advance and no security deposit. This is a matter of death; monetary considerations are unbecoming in such a situation."

Then, patting Ashok's back lightly, he asked, "I liked your candour in the advertisement."

"I would not be able to face you if I carried a dying man into your house without your knowledge. You could deny us entry and we would be on the road. We have been thrown out once before. My present landlord is waiting to see us out of his house. Death is the last visitor anyone wants to ever see in their house."

"Yet, that is the very reason I lost no time in making contact. My rooms have been lying vacant for a long time and I had no plan to lease them out. I would do so only under special circumstances, and that chance has offered itself now. Well, my home is here to welcome death, if that is what you are bringing along with you. Everyone has to die one day, some sooner than later." He twirled his moustache harder and let off a long sneeze as if in attestation of what he said.

"Go get your family, the dinner is on me tomorrow when you move in."

Was it real or was he daydreaming? Ashok pinched his thigh from within the pockets of his trousers to confirm that he was not hallucinating. He shook the Sardar's hand so hard that his own started to ache and tears of gratitude rolled down his cheeks. He ran out of the house almost delirious with joy that his dear father would not die on the street but in the very congenial environs of an extraordinary man. He cried aloud, to the surprise of the passersby, "Jo bole so nihal, sat sri akal!"

Reaching home in a fit of excitement, Ashok rushed to his dying father and gently shook him out of his stupor.

"We are returning home tomorrow, father," he spoke in his ear.

Brij Nath opened his eyes, looked at his son in bewilderment, and closed them again.

"We are going home, father" Ashok repeated.

"Home, home…" mumbled his father and relapsed into delirium.

Next day, the family moved to Nanak Nagar and, for the first time in many months, stretched their limbs that were cramped in the hellhole that they were living in. It was sometime after they had settled down that Ashok's mother threw a window open and saw a pomegranate tree in bloom in the front garden. The sight animated her. She called her son and asked him to seat his father in a chair and bring it near the window.

"We are home. That is your pomegranate tree. Look at those red flowers in bloom," she pointed to the tree.

Brij Nath lifted his head and opened his eyes. She pointed at the tree again. He looked confused. She lifted his right arm and held it across the window. Gently, she pulled a flower-laden branch of the tree to his hand. He fondled a flower—the familiar inflorescence, the smooth shiny tubular base with vermilion petals at the top. A strange light shone in his eyes and a flicker of a smile appeared on his lips before he passed out again.

On his dark and yellow face, now assuming a light vermilion hue like the flower he touched, there was contentment, the same contentment that he had worn as a motif of plain-living all his life.

8
ABDUL HAMEED'S UNEASE

The seventies and the eighties witnessed a construction boom in Kashmir. A growing and upbeat middle class started moving out from their ancestral homes, on the banks of the Jehlum in the old city down the seven bridges, to inhabit large suburban tracts of land around the periphery of the capital city of Srinagar. The idea of moving from a place where one has lived for generations can be daunting. It is not an easy decision to abandon the cloistered life in ancestral homes, the lifelong associations, the joint families, and the security of living in well-knit communities. However, with the pace of development and the population boom, people had no choice but to fan out. Kashmiri Pandits set the trend and Muslims followed suit. Barzalla, Bemina, Indira Nagar, Rawalpora, Rajbagh and others joined the ranks of an ever growing list of suburbs. The new settlements assumed a variegated hue, a blend of the majority Muslim community and the minority Pandits, with a sprinkling of Sikhs. By and large, the religious diversity of the ancient city was reproduced, except for a few predominantly single-community clusters.

Professor Shankar Nath Zutshi was one among the many who purchased a plot of land in the early eighties in a fledgling suburb on a swathe of land between the new and the old airport roads, where several Pandit families had already settled. They named it Asha Puri, The Town of Hope. A couple of the professor's Muslim colleagues also purchased plots in this neighborhood, starting a trickle of Muslim settlers which soon progressed to a steady stream. The peasants who sold their land and the middlemen who brokered the deals made huge amounts of money as the land rush and the construction boom picked up momentum.

Once there was a sizeable Muslim presence in Asha Puri, it was a foregone conclusion that a Hindu sounding name was untenable. The place was rechristened Parray Pur, after the Parrays, a family of local landlords. Though the Pandits continued to call it Asha Puri for quite some time, it did not cut much ice and they had to give in. It was not long before the name Parray Pur was endorsed by the postal, revenue and municipal authorities. Official confirmation of the name was a mere formality. This name changing followed the pattern in other neighborhoods and landmarks in Kashmir upon which Islamic names were being slapped systematically. In the process, several town squares and streets, hills and hamlets assumed new names—a concerted effort to erase local history to suit the resurgent Muslim sensibilities. It was no different from the coerced conversions of Hindus down the centuries under Muslim rule in Kashmir. But, even as the Hindu names were being wiped out, they left their genetic footprints on the acquired names. Thus we have Bhats, Kauls, Pandits, Dars and so many other

Hindu surnames surviving among the Muslims to this day.

One of the new settlers in Parray Pur was a police officer by the name of Abdul Hameed. He was quite influential by virtue of being connected to a prominent political family of Kashmir. He chose a large tract of land that flanked one side of the main entrance road to Parray Pur, a few plots away from where it forked from the highway, adjoining Professor Shankar Nath's plot. He was greedy by disposition and possessive by habit. The spoils of corruption that came his way by virtue of his profession were not enough. Police duty had made him at once overbearing and obsequious, depending upon whom he was dealing with. He was rough and gruff with the lower rung officials and menials but almost servile with his senior officers. He did not brook intrusions into his privacy and was happy to be an across-the-window neighbour. It suited him to share a common wall with the genial professor on one side and a plot earmarked for a Children's Park on the other, that gave him an unhindered view of the distant mountains. He constructed a bungalow in style and settled down to a life of comfort in the new milieu. His family got on well with the professor and his wife. The professor, who had taught two generations of students, was a private person, unobtrusive and obliging, not given to debate or discussion on controversial topics. His wife, a teacher in the Government high school at Ompura, was just the opposite—outgoing, lively, energetic, and a chatterbox. She ran the house, made all the decisions, did most of the talking and was bold and unafraid to speak her mind.

As the suburb grew, Abdul Hameed felt an unease that he could not quite explain to himself. Something irked him, and he soon figured it out. Construction was going at a fast pace. There was a lot of movement of trucks back and forth carrying building material for the homes that were being built in the neighbourhood. The trucks had to pass by his house to go deeper into the settlement. Most of the settlers inside were Pandits. He did not like them accessing their plots through the street to which he wanted exclusive rights. How dare they drive and pass everyday by his house when they could take a detour from another road forking further ahead from the highway. Surely, it wouldn't hurt them if they took a slightly longer route as long as they left him in peace, he decided.

Without giving it a second thought, and without any qualms whatsoever, Abdul Hameed laid rolls of barbed wire on the street along the fence that marked the boundary of his land. The street narrowed considerably in this segment. Cars could barely pass now and trucks had no chance. The residents requested him to remove the encroachment and let the construction material pass, but it was no use arguing with this man. He had made up his mind. He was only reinforcing his house and garden wall against any wild hits by the trucks and was within his municipal rights, he asserted. They were free to use the alternate lane if they faced problems, he reminded them.

There was no point in taking-cudgels with the obdurate Mr Hameed. Since he was a police officer with high connections, the Pandits quietly swallowed the insult.

However, Abdul Hameed's unease did not abate with this first triumph. The sight of Pandits going in and out of the suburb in their cars or on foot, while he watched from his window, did not sit well with him. This had to be stopped. It was all right to have a Pandit professor as your next-door neighbour but too many of them passing by your house all day long was more than he could bear. After a couple of months, he stuck several thick poles four feet high across the street at the end of his plot to block all vehicular traffic. Cars could no longer pass through, nor could you ride a bicycle without getting into a skirmish with the poles. Only pedestrians could use the street henceforth.

Still smarting under the earlier move that hindered their passage on this thoroughfare, the barrier caused by the poles across the road was a great blow to the Pandits. They feared that Abdul Hameed might take the next step and wall off the road making it a dead end beyond his house. Something had to be done to stop this egregious control of public property—a high utility access road at that. They approached him in a group, asking him to lift the embargo. But he was amenable neither to reason nor to their plea. It infuriated him when they threatened to petition the authorities. He dared them to knock at any official or legal door, warning them that he would block the road for pedestrian traffic as well, if they made too much fuss.

There seemed no other way than direct action. The Pandits got together in strength one night and started knocking down the poles and removing the wire mesh. Abdul Hameed would not take this outrage lying down. He engaged the services of the hoodlums of the village and got the protesting Pandits thrashed. They beat a retreat and the poles were stuck back in place, more securely than before.

The Pandits lodged a formal complaint with the local police. The inspector refused to register a case against an officer of his own department. He cautioned them that it was futile and even hazardous to take up cudgels against an influential person like Abdul Hameed. They went in a delegation to the Inspector General of Police who sent an official for spot inspection and, having verified the facts, issued an order for the removal of all impediments and encroachments and restoration of full vehicular traffic on the road. Alas, there was no one to implement the order. The inspector dithered, for he feared a backlash. Abdul Hameed was quite capable of creating a law and order problem if the encroachments were forcibly removed, he warned the Pandits. If they wanted communal harmony, they should not insist on reopening the entry road for vehicular traffic, he advised.

When the word 'communal' was thrown in, the Pandits swallowed yet another bitter pill and reconciled themselves to using the detour, hoping someday some miracle would open the regular road for them. Such bullying of Pandits was a developing trend, a sign of the growing religious chauvinism and political thuggery in Kashmir. Islamic militancy gave it a boost.

Life returned to relative tranquility for Abdul Hameed. His victory was total and final. He enjoyed his smoke sitting near his window, coughing phlegm and spitting it out onto the empty street. There were no pangs of conscience in carrying on friendly terms with his next-door Pandit neighbour, the professor, who, though not directly affected, felt very hurt by his blatant hostility to his co-religionists. But there was no escape. He could not wish his neighbor away and had no choice but to get along with him.

But peace did not last long—neither in the valley nor with Abdul Hameed. Militancy sprang its ugly head in the late eighties and the early nineties, and religious fervour gathered momentum. Young boys from towns and villages joined the ranks of Islamic militants. Some did so voluntarily while others were coerced or coaxed and sent for arms training across the border to Pakistan Occupied Kashmir. Militants demanded men, material and money for the jihad, which they had launched against the alleged occupation of Kashmir by Indian forces. Not one voice was heard against the militants or their pernicious propaganda. For years, the media, and especially the local newspapers, had been adopting the language of the jihadis. Of late, the tone of editorials had become aggressive and blatantly hostile towards the minority communities. A strange hysteria seized the masses as they joined massive processions and shouted slogans for *Azadi*. Schools were burnt down to liberate children from the yoke of books so they could take up arms for the jihad. *Azadi* had to come first, education could wait.

And a children's park could also wait. What use is a park to the revolution when you could use the land for a mosque to propagate jihad, and for a graveyard to bury the martyrs who died fighting the Indian army? It was decided by the residents of Parray Pur that the Children's Park, flanking one side of Abdul Hameed's house, be converted into a graveyard. A mosque would be erected on one end and a *jinaza-gah* on the other.

This was a community decision. Abdul Hameed had no choice but to agree even as it soured his dreams of privacy. He watched the construction with mute anger. All funeral ceremonies from Parray Pur and neighbouring villages were now held in close proximity to his house. When a militant died, the wailing and weeping, the chest beating, the sermons and exhortations, and the fanatical proclamations blew directly into his home through a loud speaker from the mosque. But he found himself helpless. Could he raise a voice against this? Could he utter a word of disapproval? Could he even afford to remain a mute spectator? Times dictated that he participate in all the proceedings with gusto as a respected elder of Parray Pur. He had to endorse the decisions of the organizers, eulogize the deeds of the militants and shed tears at their funerals even as his inner peace was in tatters. He longed for the children's laughter that was now replaced by the cacophony of jihad.

Abdul Hameed sank into melancholia.

***

On a warm spring morning, Madam Zutshi, the professor's wife was waiting for a bus to commute to her school. When the bus arrived, there was a scramble to get in. A young boy rushed forward to clear the way for her. She recognized a tenth grade student of her school who had been absent for a long time. He looked different—a strapping adolescent, sporting a struggling moustache, taller and broader than she remembered.

"You are Gulam Nabi, aren't you?" she exclaimed.

"Yes, madam, I am your student Gulam Nabi," he answered as he got into the bus after her. He wore a Khan dress—the distinctive long shirt, shalwar and a waist coat. His voice had broken and acquired a tone of self assurance.

"Where have you been all these months? Do you know you are running low on attendance?" she asked

He looked away from her, fumbling for an answer.

"I fear you may lose the chance to appear in the upcoming tests if you do not make up," she continued. Being his form teacher, she was genuinely concerned.

"I will see you one of these days, Madam. Please pay my salaams to Professor Sahib." He bowed lightly, hurried towards the exit and alighted at the next stop. The commuters, who heard the brief dialogue between them, exchanged meaningful glances. They all seemed to know, and it suddenly dawned on Madam Zutshi too, that Gulam Nabi was missing from the school because he might have returned after a stint in the terrorist training camps in Pakistan Occupied Kashmir.

Gulam Nabi did return to school after a few days, albeit on a different mission. He gate-crashed into the office of the school Principal where a staff meeting was in progress, dashed straight at the Principal and grabbed him by his throat. A struggle ensued and, before anyone knew what was happening, the Principal's necktie came loose and his wristwatch went flying to the floor.

The teachers were shocked. Nobody said a word or made any move to stop the assailant. These days, you did that at your own peril.

Only Madam Zutshi gathered the courage to reprimand the youth. "How dare you, Gulam Nabi? Aren't you ashamed to treat the head of this school thus? What happened to your manners?"

"Please stay out of this, Madam. I respect you, but this villain deserves a shoe beating. We are engaged in jihad, putting our lives at stake for *Azadi*, but this devil is bringing shame to our revolution. What values can he impart to the students? How can we usher pure and pristine Islam in Kashmir with such teachers at the helm? That is why we prefer Madrassas to learn the tenets of our great religion. That is why I have stopped attending the school."

So saying, he let go of the Principal and left, not before warning him to mend his ways or face retribution. The red-faced Principal straightened his hair and his shirt, and limped back to his chair.

Madam Zutshi, the only non-Muslim staff member in the school, was shaken by this outrage and had no idea about the allegations made by Gulam Nabi, but the other teachers seemed to grasp their import. Dumbstruck, they eyed each other in embarrassment and left one by one.

The Principal was left alone to lick his wounds.

***

Militant activity increased in the city and the villages. There were daily clashes and killings followed by instant shutdowns and strikes. Shops were shuttered, business centers locked up, schools closed. Massive processions, with the militants openly brandishing guns, became a regular spectacle. Fear reigned and the militant youths made merry. They went about freely in the lanes and the bye-lanes, knocking at the doors of any house they chose, demanding food, men and money. The rich got away by parting with cash and food; the poor had no option but to donate a young boy or two to the jihad.

Abdul Hameed was a desirable quarry for the insurgents. Masked militants would find their way into his house, borrow his car for the night to run errands, and return the car in the morning. His pleas that he was an officer and, if found out, his job could be in jeopardy, were dismissed. They knew it was a lame excuse. It was common knowledge that quite a few police officers were sympathetic to the uprising, and some policemen had even crossed over to the terror camps in Pakistan for training. And while they were away being trained in terror, they continued to be on the payroll of the State Government.

"This is humbug," the militants scoffed at him. "Is there any functioning government worth the name here that you fear losing your job? Inshallah, we will usher in a new order and we will find a better position for you."

It was becoming increasingly embarrassing for Abdul Hameed to host the masked jihadi youth every time they fancied a good meal, easy cash or a car ride. His wife wanted to run away from this humiliation against which there was no court of law, no civil authority. But he counselled patience, for he did not want to be in the bad books of the militants who might take over the reins of power any day, nor risk his present position by taking a wrong step. It was a question of biding time and staying put.

But how long can one stay afloat astride two boats? One night the masked militants descended on him again and wanted his car. Abdul Hameed said he was down with fever, coughing and wheezing, and might need to go to the hospital if his asthma got worse. The boys argued that he could borrow the neighbour's car in that case. When he refused, they grabbed his arm and started dragging him out of his house. He called for help from the open window, from the very people who were least qualified to help him—the retired Pandit professor and his wife.

"Professor Sahib, Madam Zutshi, please come here," he shouted.

In the scuffle, the mask of one of the intruders fell off. Abdul Hameed recognized the barber's son. It was as much shock as relief. He felt exhilarated and his fear vanished when he realized that this was no anonymous demon of a militant but one of the local boys.

"Oh, is that you, Naba, my barber's son! If it were not for your father I would get you arrested at once," Abdul Hameed threatened.

"Yes, it is me. And next time, mind your tongue or we will pull it out. Don't you ever call me Naba. Have you forgotten that I am Gulam Nabi? Remember, you are addressing the Area Commander of Jammu and Kashmir Liberation Front."

Meanwhile, Madam Zutshi opened her window and shouted, "What is it, Hameed Sahib? We are coming."

The boys let go of Abdul Hameed. They were angry with him for having alerted the neighbours. His wife sat in a corner, sobbing.

"We let you off today. Next time you refuse us, you will get this straight into your wooden head," the Area Commander brandished the gun that he pulled out from his jacket. "From now on you are on our watch list. You know the punishment for betrayers, don't you?"

Abdul Hameed looked away from him towards the floor, deeply hurt and crestfallen. As the intruders were retreating, the professor and his wife appeared on the scene. Ghulam Nabi, the Area Commander, made a respectful gesture at them and left with his comrades. After all, Madam Zutshi had tutored him before he disappeared for a different tutoring in the training camps! He had not forgotten basic civilities!

"We feel so sorry, Hameed Sahib. Militancy seems to have come home to roost. You always reassured us that there were no local militants here and that Parray Pur was free of them. Now it seems you have them everywhere, right in your own backyard, including my own student, the barber's son," Madam Zutshi made bold to say.

Abdul Hameed never felt so wretched in his life with the humiliation that was heaped on him by the militants, in the presence of his wife and neighbours.

"I have no words, Madam Zutshi. That they will grow so audacious as to bite the very hands that feed them is a statement of the times we live in. Yes, you are right, no one is exempt from their dastardly ways. It is no longer the jihad we believed it to be. These boys have become rapists, thugs and looters; no more the heroes that people glorified and idolized."

The monster had turned on its creator. That, however, was hardly a consolation to the Zutshi couple. Even as they felt vindicated that the common Muslims, who abetted and encouraged militancy, would be facing its brunt one day, the incident jolted them from a false sense of security. If the militants did not spare their own mentors what fate awaited the few residual Pandits in the valley, they wondered?

***

The city was in panic following the gunning down of four Indian Air Force officers by the militants on the airport road in January 1990. Pandits of Parray Pur, like Pandits everywhere in the valley, were scared out of their wits. Death had cast its ugly shadow on the highway that led to their nests. Madam Zutshi's aunt, who had been staying with her for several months, became fidgety and nervous after the incident and urged to be sent away to Jammu where many Pandits had already fled. An army officer, who was related to the Zutshis, sent a security guard to accompany her to the airport. That was enough to put off Mrs. Hameed. She boycotted the Zutshis and stopped returning their compliments and courtesies. But Madam Zutshi was a courageous woman. The next time she saw her, she confronted her: "You seem to be avoiding us. Are you annoyed over something we are not aware of, Mrs. Hameed?" she asked.

"Come on, you know it, don't you. The way you frighten the neighbourhood with your connections with the army," Mrs. Hameed complained. "What was the need for getting an army escort for your aunt? We would not have stopped her from leaving. What use is an old Pandit woman to Kashmir?" She could not hide her contempt for the Pandits.

"Why are you sore? Are our lives less precious than yours, Mrs. Hameed. When your sister-in-law visits you, she does not come alone. There is always a posse of security guards with her. That does not seem to bother you?"

"But that is our own police, not the Indian Army," she argued.

"Yes, the same army that is making sacrifices to keep you safe from your own desperadoes." Madam Zutshi was a verbal pugilist.

The lid of a simmering distrust between the neighbours had blown up.

The killing of the Air Force officers led to an increase in police presence. A Central Reserve Force unit was stationed near Parray Pur. The locals were enraged and raised a clamour against the move. They whined that women and children were not safe with the paramilitary forces, who knew no niceties, had no respect for Muslim culture and were ruthless in frisking and, generally, humiliating the populace.

"We are peace-loving citizens and there is no need for a Central Reserve Force picket," they protested.

Ostensibly, Abdul Hameed was in the vanguard of this protest. Privately though, he and his wife were happy with the picket which came as a reprieve because the militants were thwarted in their nocturnal adventures, and their forays into the neighbourhood became few and far between. The activities in the Children's Park mosque abated to a large extent. Other Muslims were pleased with the picket as well but they dared not say so openly though they could no longer conceal their relief, some of them even making friendly overtures to the security personnel, as they passed by.

An uneasy calm prevailed. But the Zutshis were distressed at the behaviour of their belligerent neighbour. They had courageously weathered the vicissitudes of terrorism all alone, but with every passing day they felt that they could no longer take anything for granted. After retirement from the government job, Professor Shankar Nath Zutshi had accepted a part-time teaching job in a private institution, the Islamia College, to stay engaged, while his wife was still in active service. Now she too had retired. She was a restless woman. She could not stay home the whole day. Yet, she had nowhere to go to let off the steam that would build up inside her. Almost all their relatives had fled and none had returned from exile all these years. Their children—a son and a daughter—were both married and settled outside the valley. Besides, more and more Pandits of Parray Pur were selling their houses and vacant plots of land that they had purchased only a couple of years back. There was no socializing, whatsoever. Her husband's company was boring at best, tiring at worst. The Hameed couple continued their boycott.

The Zutshis had been dismissive of the pleas of their children to move out of Kashmir. Not anymore. What compelled them to accept the risk of living in Kashmir, with no one to turn to in case of an emergency, the children wanted to know. Now that both of them had retired and got their pension claims settled, there was no point staying on, They argued. The end to terrorism was nowhere in sight and the return of the exiled Pandits seemed a very remote possibility. It was in the fitness of things to wind up from Kashmir. While they were still there, they could bargain for a good price for their house, unlike the Pandits who had fled and were forced to sell in distress.

Madam Zutshi gave her children's plea serious thought and accepted the logic of their argument. But the professor was a laid-back person, loath to make major decisions. He had settled into a comfortable groove after retirement. He hated the idea of moving out of Kashmir and did not care what happened to the rest of the world, as long as he was treated well at the Islamia College. They needed his services and made him feel important. He did not feel the same way about terrorism as thousands of others who had fled. Why should he even think of moving now when the worst seemed over? In any case, during the winter months the couple regularly moved out to spend time with their children in the plains and during summer there was no place better than Parray Pur, militancy or no militancy. It was his nest, his paradise and his final retreat. He would like to spend his sunset years here even as he knew he might be the next victim of terrorism. Why, for god's sake, should they even contemplate to barter this paradise for exile? Why couldn't his impetuous wife leave him in peace?

Notwithstanding, Madam Zutshi had made up her mind, and it was she who called the shots. She also called in the brokers. Shankar Nath had no gumption to stop her. He merely acquiesced as he had done all his life.

When Abdul Hameed got wind of their plans to sell and move of Kashmir, he lost his fragile mental equilibrium yet again. He worried who his next-door neighbour might be in case the Zutshis decided to sell. He feared it might be one of the nouveau riche that terrorism had spawned, the scores of nobodies before the insurgency who had now amassed wealth and clout beyond their wildest imagination and were on a buying spree, collecting properties—someone like Naba, the barber's son-turned-militant. Abdul Hameed would not allow that under any circumstances. He must break the ice with the Zutshis, get to the bottom of this, and offer to buy their house if they planned to sell it.

One day he crossed over to meet them. Madam Zutshi was in her lawn.

"What a surprise to have you visiting, Hameed Sahib. I hope it was not by mistake," she greeted him with a mischievous smile.

He had come prepared for her banter. "Come on, Madam Zutshi, it has been a long time. We have remained good neighbours all through. Militancy has put all of us under a terrible strain. We cannot allow it to dominate our lives, nor let small misunderstandings come between us. I have come to renew our friendship."

"As far as we are concerned, we had never broken it off. We still value you as our worthy neighbours. However, it is nice of you to call. Pray, how is your asthma, how is madam?"

"My asthma is under control. Madam is fine and will be seeing you soon. Is Professor Sahib home?"

"He has gone shopping. Take a chair; I will get you a cup of tea."

"No, thanks. I will have tea some other time," he answered as he took his seat.

He did not know how to broach the subject of the house. Then, looking around, he remarked, "Looks like your porch has been damaged by the frost. The bricks are coming loose. They need attention."

"Yes, we have been delaying repairs for one reason or the other," she said. "Strangely, after my retirement, I hardly seem to get enough time."

"You are not delaying it for some other reason, are you?" He was coming to the point.

"I don't get you, Hameed Sahib," she asked, looking surprised.

"There is a rumour that you intend to sell your house and leave Kashmir like the others. I hope it is not true."

She knew he had not called without a purpose. Now it was clear.

"We have not given it any serious thought," she replied.

"You have borne the brunt of these trying times with the rest of us all these years. Now, when militancy is on the decline, there is no reason for you to leave." He was trying to probe deeper and to keep the conversation going on the subject.

"It has been a roller coaster experience, but there seems to be no end to terrorism, as long as people do not rise against it." She was always one for catching him on the wrong foot.

"The common man is caught between the devil and the deep sea," he replied.

"Pray who is the devil and who the sea?" she asked teasingly.

"The militants on the one hand, the army and the security forces on the other," he replied.

"Oh come on! that is the usual refrain of people here. But don't you agree that the devil is of your own making? If you had not encouraged the militants to take up arms, the army would not be here. Now that the uprising has been blunted, the militants have turned on you, for you are standing on the fence, neither joining the jihad openly nor condemning it. You want to have the cake and eat it too—keep militancy going and still hope to make the best of it. In the process, you have unwittingly helped destroy the fabric of the society here." She was unsparing.

He froze for a while and his anger rose at this scathing attack. How dare a Pandit woman talk to him like this? But he controlled himself, for the purpose of his visit would be lost if he retaliated.

"Yes, Kashmir is not going to be the same again. I do not know where it will end," he barely managed to speak.

"You mean militancy?" she asked.

"Yes. I realize that *Azadi* is a distant dream, but unfortunately the culture of the gun has come to stay."

"I fear you are going after a mirage and losing the *Azadi* you enjoyed before militancy raised its ugly head in Kashmir. It is never too late, Hameed Sahib; people like you have to take the lead. You have to rise against it." She was surprised at her own audacity.

He nodded in agreement, "You are right. But it is easier said than done."

There was a pause in the conversation. She had led him to a sensitive topic that the Muslims of the valley did not dare discuss freely even amongst themselves, lest they be taken as renegades and subversives She knew it was not prudent to needle him further while Abdul Hameed was keen to direct the conversation to the matter of the house again.

"You have been exemplary neighbours, Madam Zutshi. You can be assured of our support under all circumstances," he made bold to declare.

"Thanks a lot for your kind words. Yes, we need to stay together for good or for worse," she replied and again changed the topic, "care for a cup of *kehva*?"

It was hopeless to continue, he realized. "Not now. I will certainly drop in another time to savour your special *kehva*."

He rose from the chair, took her leave, walked thoughtfully halfway to the gate and returned. He had suffered more than he had bargained for when he moved into Parray Pur. He was not ready for another setback. He was determined not to let a stranger move into the Zutshi house. He must speak to her about it. Now.

"Madam Zutshi, I do hope you will stay on. But, if you ever decide to sell your house, please let us know. State the price and we will raise the money somehow."

She gave him a meaningful look. She remained non-committal, though. She was in no hurry.

Abdul Hameed's despondency and disquiet simmered. He was beset by a consuming sickness. He had successfully blocked the Pandit traffic; the militants no longer intruded his privacy; he even enjoyed local respect of sorts. But the conversion of the Children's Park into a cemetery and mosque was a stunning disappointment. His move into Parray Pur could not be termed a big success. And now, an unknown factor had entered into the delicate equation. Who would land in the Zutshi house if they decided to sell it off?

Alas, the final blow was yet to fall. The winter of 1992 set in early. It was felt by the management of the Children's Park that a mosque without a hammam was incomplete. The militants deserved a hot bath after nights of operations! There was a consensus that a hammam be constructed by the side of the mosque.

With large donations from zealots, it did not take much time for the hammam to be constructed, adjacent to Hameed's house. Every morning, bundles of firewood were fed to the furnace to heat the water. It raised serpentine coils of steam and smoke that slithered into Abdul Hameed's house, at times billowing into his living room, aggravating him and his asthma.

***

One day, the irrepressible Madam Zutshi chanced to meet Abdul Hameed on the highway while she was waiting for a bus to the city. Just then he was having a long bout of coughing.

"Your cough seems to have grown worse of late, Hameed Sahib?" She looked at him inquiringly.

"It will pass, Madam Zutshi. I feel it is the early onset of winter that caught me unawares."

"Or, maybe the smoke?" She eyed him mischievously.

"Smoke?" He exclaimed. "Did I not tell you that I have given up smoking these five weeks?"

"Well, that is good to hear. It will help your asthma. However, I was speaking about the smoke from the chimney," she said with a chuckle.

"The chimney?" he exclaimed.

"The chimney of the hammam in the Children's Park," she quipped.

"Oh I see! but it does not really matter," he replied in embarrassment.

"True, the early onset of winter may not be easy on your cough but the hammam, so close, almost hugging your house, must provide some warmth as well?"

But he had touched a new low and did not have the nerve to react to that biting sarcasm.

"Come on, don't taunt me, sister; you really sound naughty today."

She felt encouraged to say more than she should have. She had waited her chance to hit him back for his insolence and arrogance. There could be no better occasion than when he addressed her as sister.

"Of course this is a different ballgame, not the same as blocking the road to the suburb. In any case, Hameed Sahib, it seems the roadblock that you enforced may soon become meaningless. Several Pandit families have fled. Some have left their constructions incomplete, others have not even moved into their newly-built homes and yet others are finding buyers for their plots. One day you may have the whole street, nay, the whole Parray Pur to yourself. No longer will you need to feel sore about Pandits passing the street by your house. Once their properties are sold off you will be forced to open the road to traffic again. Others who move in will not wait for an Inspector General of Police to issue an order that never gets implemented."

"You are right. It is the curse of the Pandits that haunts us." He seemed remorseful for the first time since she knew him.

"Once all the Pandits are gone, there will be no one to bash, Hameed Sahib?"

"You are not going, are you? You are not leaving us to face an uncertain future alone?"

"To you your *Azadi*, to us our freedom," she remarked.

"Now, what does that mean, Mrs Zutshi?"

But she hurried on to board the bus and left him perplexed.

***

There was no escape from the smoke coming from the chimney breathing into Abdul Hameed's house, or from the traffic which resumed on the street that he had blocked. Worse, a new neighbour had moved into the Zutshi house.

It is said that, for a long time now, Abdul Hameed has neither opened the window overlooking the road nor the window from where he would exchange pleasantries with the Zutshis. As to the unobstructed view of the distant hills that he longed for, well, the high chimney of the hammam in the Children's Park stands in the way.

9
GULLA OF PRANG

(I)

An hour's drive northeast of the city of Srinagar, the Sindh Valley unfolds its treasure trove of religious, archaeological and scenic spots. There is Khirbhavani, the seat of the most exalted deity of Kashmiri Pandits, barely twenty five kilometers away. Manasbal, a little jewel of a limpid turquoise lake, nesting quietly amid the mountains is six kilometers from there. Another twenty minutes drive into the hills, and you are at Naran Nag, an archaeological gem with its ruins of an ancient Hindu temple-complex. This is also the base camp for pilgrimage to Gangabal, a high altitude lake, twelve thousand feet above the sea. Pandits trek there in the month of September to immerse the ashes of their dead and perform shraddha for their departed ancestors. Prang is a pretty village in the lap of the Sindh Valley on the bank of the river Sindh, midway between Khirbhavani and Naran Nag.

Prang has been a favourite retreat for my family for its sheer beauty and proximity to the city. The mountains are close, the woods deep, and the river, a wide sheet of water running merrily on a clear stone-bed along the village. Whenever we planned a visit, we started with Khirbhavani and drove to Manasbal on the way to Prang.

Prang is dear to my heart for another reason. It gave us a family friend. It happened during a short holiday in the month of August in 1983. We were driving to Prang when my Ambassador suffered a puncture, just as we reached the village. I pulled over to the side, cranked up the jack, and started easing the wheel out when a shy, slightly built young man with a sparse moustache climbed down from a shop that had been created from the front of a ramshackle hut. I had not noticed him approach the car until I saw him standing behind me. And then, gently taking the wheel away from me, he said in a soft voice, "Jenab, allow me," and replaced it. I did not know what to say; he acted as if I was doing him a favour.

He lowered the jack, put it away in the trunk along with the punctured tyre, rushed to his shop to fetch a jug of water and helped me wash my hands. He went through the whole exercise as if he were performing a duty.

"Thank you; what is your name?" I asked, wiping my hands while my wife and children looked on with fascination.

"Ghulam Mohammad. You can call me Gulla."

"Do you belong here, Gulla?"

"Yes, this is my home and work place as well."

"What do you do?"

"I am a tailor."

"You should be in school; you are too young to be working."

"You are right, Jenab. But I did not have a choice. Circumstances forced me to fend for myself before I could complete my education."

"Well, thank you again. How can we show our gratitude to you, Gulla?"

"Where are you heading, Jenab? Please come in and grace my humble home; that would please me," and then turning to Leela, "pray come in madam; the girls might like a cup of fresh milk from our own cow."

"Thank you; may be some other time," she replied, giving him a maternal pat on his back.

"We will be here in Prang for a couple of days. Who knows we may even decide someday to settle in your lovely village," I said, not quite seriously.

"I hope you are not making fun of me. Our fortunes will smile if you come to stay here." There was no pretence in his voice.

"Well, we will take up your invitation some other time. For now we will be staying close by in the rest house," I said, starting the car. He waved enthusiastically as we drove away. It was around noon.

The Prang rest house, perched on the edge of the river, is surrounded by sprawling lawns. We took our baggage out of the trunk and lugged it inside. Soon after, we spread a dhurrie under a Chinar and ate a hearty lunch, serenaded by the sweet music of the river and enraptured by the beauty of the hills. A family of crows flew over and perched on a tree nearby. A couple of dogs hovered around, eyeing the dishes, waiting for leftovers.

Soon after lunch, we removed our shoes, rolled up our trousers and waded into the clear, ice-cold stream till our feet got numb. Sitting on boulders, we watched the trout flitting across the riverbed, positioning themselves in the face of the current, their mouths wide open to receive the grub that the racing stream brought with it. We spent hours wading in the river and walking on the green lawn. Before we knew it, the sun began to go down and we watched the sky in its multihued splendour and the clouds in myriad formations, till the hush of night started to descend on the sleepy village.

We moved to the patio, and watched the magical closing ceremony of the day, lapping up the cool breeze that blew across the river to send a delicious chill, when Gulla materialized. He wore a loose pheron over the shirt and shalwar that he had worn earlier in the day. He was carrying a copper bowl covered with a white towel in his hands. I had forgotten him in the excitement of the evening, yet how welcome he was!

"Salaam Jenab," he said, bowing respectfully, gingerly placing the bowl on a table, shy and almost stammering, "I do not know if you will like this."

"What is it, Gulla?" I asked

"Jenab, these are corn rotis, a specialty of Prang. My mother made them."

"But we just met by chance, you helped me replace the wheel and beyond that you don't even know us. We have done nothing to deserve this honour."

"Does it matter who you are, when my heart tells me that you are nice people that I should make friends with?" He was spontaneous, sincere.

Turning towards Leela, he said, "I do not know whether you partake of food cooked by Muslims, but I can assure you these rotis have been made with great care."

"You overwhelm us with your indulgence, Gulla. We are unorthodox, not fastidious about food. Besides, how can we refuse your offering of love?" she said reassuringly.

These rotis had been made from freshly milled corn flour and baked on the upturned curved bottom of a large clay pot, on a flame of pine needles. The wafer thin rotis were the largest that we had ever seen. They seemed so rustic, so original.

"I don't know what made you think of corn rotis, Gulla. It so happens that we love them. Tell us how you make them so thin and yet so round and large. How do you prevent the dough from breaking up when it is spread and rolled?" Leela asked.

"It is easy, madam; needs a bit of practice and patience. We make it with bare hands, no roller plate, no pin. It comes naturally to us. You will have to come to our house and watch mother do it," he urged.

"I will before we leave. This is art born of passion. To do it for someone you do not even know speaks of a generous heart. Please thank your mother on our behalf."

There were more than a dozen rotis. It must have taken his mother quite an effort. They had the delightful pristine taste of virgin corn.

He watched us apply ourselves to his rotis, at first with some trepidation as if he were waiting to hear the result of a test. When he saw us lapping them up, he smiled gratefully.

"Who else is in your family?" Leela asked.

"My old father, and ..." he hesitated for a moment, blushed, and looking away from her, continued almost in a whisper, "my wife."

"So you are married? Where is your wife?"

"She has gone to her parents' home. It is in the next village." He was shy, avoiding eye contact.

"You certainly seem rather young to be married."

"My mother is getting old. She wanted someone to help her with the household chores and married me to a distant cousin. We have a small landholding that does not produce enough to sustain the family. I could not pursue my studies beyond the fifth grade. Father managed to buy me a sewing machine. I worked as an apprentice for a few months before I converted the room facing the street into a shop."

"Do you have kids?"

"Not yet; I hope they don't come for some time. It was a mistake to marry young though it is common in the villages here." He fell silent.

That was the whole life story of this village youth. Or was it?

We promised to meet his family and to thank his mother in person. He did not ask any questions, as if he knew everything about us. I thought it fit to tell him that both of us were doctors, that we worked at the Medical College Hospital in Srinagar, that our two daughters were high school students, that our parents lived with us, that we lived at Barbarshah near the temple, that if he ever needed help he was welcome to ask us.

Next morning, I was up before the others and sauntered off for a walk in the hills. The pines seemed unusually scarce near the foothills. I was shocked to find numerous stumps left behind from pines that had been felled randomly. Worse, several standing pines were shorn of all the branches except near the top, and many others had been debarked and left with wounds and gashes. There was scarce undergrowth, and the hills looked almost bare. It was a tragic sight. When the sun rose, there was hardly enough shade to make you feel you were in a forest. I had a feeling of profound sadness as I returned to the Rest House to find Gulla loitering in the lawn. He wore a clean shirt and a short jacket, his hair well oiled and combed back, and a confident smile playing on his face.

He wished me a good morning and asked, "Jenab, where had you been so early? Did you go around our village?"

"No, I was in the woods, whatever is left of them. I found stumps everywhere. The pines that have been spared the axe, stand like poles of timber shorn of their branches and foliage. Others have been debarked over the whole length of their trunks. Tell me, Gulla, who has wrought this devastation to the jungle? It used to be a dense forest here."

"Jenab, it is a tragic tale. The forest lessees, in connivance with the officials, cut the pines indiscriminately to rob the wealth of the woods. Poor villagers cut the branches of the standing trees for fuel."

"But why skin the poor trees alive? Who benefits from this vandalism? They must be without a heart to commit such barbarity." I got rather emotional.

"It is the village folk. Last year we had a large team of government officials here, after they received reports of indiscriminate cutting down of pines. Additional forest guards were posted. That slowed it down somewhat, but did not eliminate the illegal felling and chopping of branches. Now the wily villagers have found a novel way of attack. During nights, unheard and unseen, they quietly strip off the bark of the healthy pines. Over a period of time the denuded trees wither away, rot, and fall down. Written off as dead by the forest staff, the villagers fall upon the remains like vultures. No cutting, no poaching, no big fuss; just a quiet death and no tears shed! 'The fox takes the meat, the dog get the hide,' goes the saying." Gulla could not hide his disgust.

It pained me to hear the story of the wounded forest. "Why do you deprive yourselves of the bounties of nature? Why are the villagers bent on converting this paradise into a desert? Is there nobody who can stop this destruction? Can I have a word with the forest ranger?" I asked.

"It will be no use, Jenab. They are in it together, from the top to the bottom—the forest guards, the ranger, the divisional forest officer, the conservator and the minister. They all get a share of the loot. You should know it better than me."

For the rest of the morning I was in a daze, imagining the worst possible scenarios for Kashmir—the hills denuded of trees, the water in the rivers at rock bottom, the lakes drying up, the green pastures laid to waste, weeds taking over. I woke up with a shudder, my heart racing, mouth parched, sweat on my brow. No, this devastation had to stop!

We spent the day near the river and played games in the lawn but it was not the same as the previous day. In the evening, we walked along the street and met Gulla in his shop. He was expecting us and asked us in.

We were led to a small mud-plastered room with bare walls, a grass-mat covering the floor, two pillows lining one of the walls, and his father in a dark-grey woollen *pheron* and a cotton skullcap pulling at a hookah in one corner. We exchanged greetings and sat near him. Gulla placed the pillows behind us. His mother entered soon after. Lightly freckled and deeply wrinkled, she wore a green *pheron*, a *qasaba* on her head, heavy metal bangles, and two large silver ear rings dangling from long slits in her ear lobes, threatening to split them. I thanked her for the rotis and praised her skill. She showed us the hearth and the large clay pot on which she baked them.

"It must take a lot of effort?" Leela asked.

"But it is worth the toil. Both of you are doctors, so my son told me, and it might sound arrogant on my part, but cooking in clay pots is the best thing. It preserves the taste of food and it does not pollute or poison the food as metallic vessels do. God made and shaped us out of clay and clay is sacred to all—to Pandits and Muslims alike. There is nothing like earthenware for cooking rice or meat. Pandits in this village cook the tastiest potato dish, the damaloo, for their sons-in-law in earthen pots."

We thanked her again, praised her son for his winsome ways, salaamed respectfully and took our leave.

The holiday ended and we returned home the next morning. Gulla waved us off. It was a sad parting, but the beginning of a strong bond with this village lad who wanted to be friends, just for the sake of friendship.

Gulla showed up some days later at our residence and kept visiting us every so often. He invariably brought with him some seasonal gifts from the village—roasted rice seeds, fresh corn flour, green walnuts, almonds, corn cobs, apples, and cherries—that we relished both for the taste and the love that was packed in them. He hardly ever asked a favour, and made friends with everyone in our home, especially my mother with whom he would share details of his life in the village. He became part of our family.

Gulla was nineteen and married for two years. Soon after marriage, his wife Jana had found employment in the Anganwadi scheme. Young and immature as she was, her job as a State Government employee had turned her head and she had started putting on airs, flaunting her status to the family, even though she was the lowest functionary in her workplace. She treated Gulla with indifference, sometimes with contempt, for being just a lowly tailor. He was too young, too proud and too meek to retaliate. He bore her taunts with equanimity but when she ran to her parents' home on one flimsy excuse or the other, it saddened him. People ridiculed him, asked difficult questions that made him feel worthless and wretched.

The first time we met him at Prang, Jana had gone to her parents' home in one of those huffs. But Gulla was too proud to tell us then. Now it came out slowly and we understood the reason for the faraway look in his eyes, his sad demeanor, and his diffidence. I felt sorry for the lad; I had no idea how to help him.

Once, when Jana was gone to her parents for more than a month, Gulla chose to visit us. It was a Sunday and I was tending roses in my garden when he entered and salaamed. I could see something was amiss. He wore a long face, his eyes sadder than ever. I missed his wonderful smile and asked him if all was well with him. Yes, all was well, he replied; he had just come to say hello. After some time he went inside to confide to my mother the problems he was having with his wife and how she had walked out on him again. There was no precipitating cause, just one of her tantrums. It was getting worse with every new episode.

"Does she desire someone else," my mother ventured to ask.

"No, she is honourable and I can vouch for her fidelity. She just feels I am good for nothing, not worthy of her," Gulla stated wistfully.

"But she is married to you for good and for bad and she must stick with you. Where will she find a faithful, loving husband like you?" Mother asked.

"I fear that is not so. I am no good; I am just a poor village tailor. All I can stitch together is a *pheron* for the village folks, a simple shirt

or an ordinary shalwar. I cannot even stitch a good blouse for her."
He seemed disappointed with himself.

"You are an intelligent man; you will get better with time. You are
still very young; she must be even younger. I am sure she will wake up
to your good qualities as she matures. Why don't you bring her here
one of these days and I will speak to her?" Mother was quite indulgent.

"Jana has an unpredictable temper; she may not agree to come
here. I have become a laughing stock in the village. Even my parents
ridicule me at times. They blame me for not being able to tame her. I
am not like the others who beat their wives into submission. Besides,
she is educated. What will the world think?"

"Educated? What level of education?" Mother asked.

"She has passed the eighth grade."

He was taken by surprise when mother burst into laughter.

"That is not a lot of education. There is not much difference
between your fifth grade and her eighth. I agree, women should be
treated with respect. Yet, they must know right from wrong. They
must accept their duty towards home and husband. I advise you to
visit her and take her parents into confidence."

"If I call on my in-laws she may insult me in their presence. That
will be worse than death for me. I do not want to face her parents. I
hope she will return one day on her own. I will wait for her."

"Do her parents approve of you?"

"They did, that is why we were married."

"They should send her back. A daughter has no place with
her parents once she is married. Her home is with her in-laws and
husband."

"I wish she would understand that," he sighed.

"Have you ever spoken about us to her?" Mother asked.

"Yes, I have told her about your family. Some time back, she wanted to come here to be examined by madam doctor for a gynaecological problem. But before I could bring her here, we had a small argument on a trivial matter and she flew into rage and ran to her parents."

"Well, go tell her we are keen to see her. I want to give her my blessings. Don't be afraid. Be a man," Mother cheered him up.

When he returned home after visiting us, Gulla steeled his resolve, put his reticence aside, and went to his in-laws to extend our invitation to his estranged wife. To his great surprise, it worked. Jana returned home with him.

One afternoon, a couple of weeks later, Gulla, accompanied by his wife, called on us. Nicely dressed in an embroidered frock, a scarf covering her head and neck, silver bangles jingling on her slender arms, Jana looked very petite and pretty.

We indulged them, lavished pleasantries on her, and treated Gulla with deference, putting him at ease, making him feel important. After tea, I called Gulla out in the garden. Jana stayed back in the living room with Mother while Leela started her evening clinic.

Nearly an hour later, mother accompanied Jana to Leela's room and said, "Jana needs to be given a check up. She is shy; that is why I am with her."

Leela examined her and heaped a bag of nutritional supplements on her, and a lot of affection. Just before dusk, the couple took our leave. Jana salaamed us respectfully and gave a parting hug to mother. She seemed happy.

Winter announced itself early that year. On a Sunday, while we were harnessing the heating stoves in the living room, Gulla made a quiet entrance. All of us besieged him with questions as I realized how we had missed him.

He wore a wide smile on his childlike face that I had come to like so much. He had come to tell us that his wife was transformed beyond his expectations. She now helped in the household chores and took interest in Gulla's tailoring and treated him with respect. He was a different man now, full of confidence, full of the desire to prove himself worthy of this change in his wife. No longer was he the butt of ridicule in the village. His standing had improved as his clientele increased slowly and so did his working hours that sometimes ran late into the night, especially during Eid when people ordered new clothes.

He sought Mother and sat near her. "It is all because of you, Mother; I do not know how to thank you. Your words were like commandments to her."

Then he turned to address Leela, "Doctor Sahiba, you must have given her a magic potion."

"What? Do you have any good news?" she asked.

He blushed. "Yes, Jana is in the family way. I am going to be a father!"

(II)

Alas, this land of sages, savants and seers fell on bad times. Terrorism erupted in the late eighties and struck at the very heart of the ethos of Kashmir. It tore apart the delicate fabric of harmony between communities.

Gulla did not turn up for a long time, nor did we get an opportunity to visit Prang. Father was struck with cancer. He passed away in the spring of 1989. When fall arrived, we decided to visit Gangabal. It would serve the twin purposes of a hiking trip, long overdue, as well as a pilgrimage. We planned to immerse father's ashes in the sacred waters of the lake. On our way, we also hoped to catch up with Gulla at Prang.

We started late in the day and reached Prang in the evening. Gulla's shop was closed. Since we had to start early the next morning, we decided to see him on our return from Gangabal. Staying in the familiar rest house, we came out after dinner for our customary stroll in the lawns. We hoped to lend our ear to the silences of the woods and the song of the river, but what we saw was unsettling. A group of young boys was engaged in some sort of drill, not unlike military exercises. They turned to look at us, but their instructor shouted at them to get back into the drill. His voice was stern, his looks intimidating. This was no time for such activity; these boys should have been with their books, or in bed. We cut short our stroll and returned to the rest house.

I felt uneasy and could not sleep that night. We had knowledge that young boys from the city and the villages were being inducted into Jihad. We had been witness to shots fired randomly at different places in the city. There were rumours of an insurgency breaking out; of young boys disappearing from villages, absent from their schools for weeks and months and their parents not complaining or revealing their whereabouts; of busloads of young aspirants for Jihad heading to the border town of Uri from where they crossed over to Pakistan Occupied Kashmir. Now, unbeknown to the world outside, kids were being trained for some sort of uprising right under our noses. It was very disturbing to realize that the lawns of the rest house at Prang had been turned into a training ground for militants.

Next morning, during the arduous climb up the Buthsher range, I quizzed Maqbool about what we had seen the previous night. Maqbool hailed from Kurihama, a few kilometers from Prang. Like Gulla, he was another family friend and a frequent visitor to our home. He had arranged the hiking trip for us. He confirmed that these were village lads who had been recruited for militancy and were being trained in subversion and guerrilla warfare. Some of them had returned from across the border after receiving training and were now instructing the local youth in the use of bombs, grenades and guns.

We must have been about midway when the weather turned rough unexpectedly. Dense fog appeared as if by magic, black clouds came rolling by, and soon it was dark at noon. It started pouring and we almost lost each other in the fog and the blinding rain. It was with great difficulty that we stayed intact during the night as strong winds lashed at us and blew the tent away. The pilgrimage was a washout and seemed ominous, an indication of what was to come—the bad times that would fall upon the people of Kashmir.

We returned the next day, walking through pools of mud, slipping and sliding in pouring rain that drenched us to the skin. We halted several times and took shelter in Gujjar kothas to rest and recuperate, reaching Naran Nag late in the evening. The mules that we had engaged refused to take us any further. A kindly Gujjar offered us a room for the night but right then, we stopped an approaching truck and the driver agreed to take us to Prang.

We reached Prang late, at eleven in the night. We could have stayed for the night in the rest house and met Gulla the next morning but the whole trip had left us drained of energy and enthusiasm, fearful of what was in store in the coming days. There was a foreboding of evil. Besides, Mother would have been very worried about our safety in this terrible weather. Heavy rain had washed away houses and swallowed many hamlets. There was no point halting here after the hiking trip that had turned into a nightmare.

It was past midnight when we reached home, to the great relief and joyous tears of Mother.

We were not destined to meet Gulla in Kashmir again.

(III)

Nine years later, on a cold December day in Jammu, I am in my surgery, examining patients.

There is a crowd in the waiting room, mainly Kashmiri Pandit refugees afflicted with all kinds of ailments, physical and psychological, caused as a result of the displacement from their homes in Kashmir and the vicissitudes of exile. They are waiting patiently for their turn. There are also some Muslim patients from Kashmir. They have no previous appointments, having arrived a day or two earlier from the valley. They want to be examined as early as possible so they can return home without having to spend a day longer in the hotels. But the receptionist is dismissive of their pleas for there are no openings for a whole week.

The patients from Kashmir remonstrate, "Can't you see, we have sick patients with us who cannot wait another day?"

"In that case you should go to the emergency department of the government hospital which is open all hours," he retorts.

They are furious. They have come all the way from Kashmir to consult me and not to be dismissed and directed to the government hospital, they remind him. But he is not impressed.

A burly bearded Muslim growls, "Have a heart, Panditji; my father is in a terrible state. I got him here at great risk. He almost collapsed on the way when we were held up at Banihal. He will die waiting a whole week in the hotel. If anything happens to him, you will be responsible."

"Don't pressure me, mister. No bullying here, understand? This is not Kashmir where you used to browbeat us. I have not invited you here. Are there no doctors left in the valley?" The receptionist is uncompromising.

"Yes there are but we have come all the way to be seen by your doctor and not by anyone else, because we trust him." His swagger disappears, his tone softens.

"In that case, you should not have driven your favourite doctor out of Kashmir along with all the Pandit population," the receptionist castigates him.

"Please don't blame us; it was Governor Jagmohan who lured you out of Kashmir."

"Lured us to this hell here, to the tents and tenements, to the heat and the dust, to the snakes and scorpions?" the receptionist retorts back.

"There were some unsavoury elements, I agree, who brought this tehrik a bad name," the bearded man suddenly sounds apologetic.

"Call it *tafreek*, not *tehrik*. Yes, your militancy is a pestilence, not a *tehrik*, not a freedom movement. What freedom are you fighting for that were denied to you? Was anyone stopping you from offering prayers, from building your mosques, from operating madrassas where you breed terrorists? You have been living off the blood and sweat of millions of Indians?" The receptionist is unsparing.

The bearded fellow raises his arms, palms supine, and looks to the ceiling in an invocatory gesture, "Death to the ruffians who brought Kashmir to this pass! They are now reaping their just rewards. Inshallah, old times will be back again."

Then he makes a fresh plea, "Please, let the doctor see my father today."

The Pandit refugees are watching with great interest, amazed at the receptionist's retorts, even admiring his candour. Back home in Kashmir, they could never have imagined a Pandit arguing with such forcefulness with a Muslim. Nevertheless, their inherent fondness for fellow Kashmiris surfaces even in their adversity. That is what prompts an elderly, soft-spoken Pandit to intervene on behalf of the visitor from the valley, and plead with the receptionist.

"Let his father take my turn, please; his need appears more urgent than mine. After all, they are our own Kashmiri brethren. The golden chains of amity between us may have come under strain but are not irretrievably broken. There is still a lot of goodwill left."

The receptionist relents, "All right, I will do my best and try to accommodate him today. There is no acrimony, no ill-will; I was only speaking my mind."

Peace supervenes.

Watching this exchange, and waiting with great impatience to get a chance with the receptionist is another Muslim in his thirties, sporting a shirt and a woollen vest. He is calm in demeanor and approaches the receptionist with great humility.

"I am not a patient, Panditji. I have just come to meet Doctor Sahib."

"Pray, what have you come to meet him for?" The receptionist cannot suppress his sarcasm.

"Just to say my salaams, and pay him my respects," he answers gently.

"As you can see, the doctor is very busy. You can say your salaams after he is through with the patients."

"Jenab, looking at the crowd of patients waiting here, it may take him the whole morning and part of the afternoon. I do not have much time. I have to take the return bus to Kashmir tomorrow; I have to meet him today. That is all I came to Jammu for. Give me a minute-please. Tell him, a man from Prang is here to see him."

"Listen my dear young fellow, these people here have been waiting their turn to see the doctor for some time now. I cannot let you in ahead of them. Why don't you return later, say around 1-30 PM?" The overstretched receptionist is trying to be accommodative.

It is no use arguing with the receptionist. The man from Prang thinks of a way out. He stands in front of the door to my chamber, hoping that I might catch a glimpse of him standing there as the patients move in and out of the chamber.

He keeps waiting there for quite some time without any success. Finally, as a patient walks out of the chamber, the door opens wide for another patient, a paralytic, who is being wheeled in. Just then, the man from Prang cranes his neck and my eyes fall on him.

Suddenly, the distinct flavour of a distant past and a far-away place wafts in. I fumble for a name, a place. I am about to dismiss the thought when I hear him greeting me aloud, "Salaam, Doctor Sahib".

There is no mistaking now. That gentle voice, etched in my memory, can belong to none other. That certainly is Gulla of Prang, the tailor, impatient to squeeze his way in.

I signal to him to wait. His face falls, his beaming smile fades away quickly as he withdraws and the door closes.

Memories rush in. I cannot concentrate on the new patient. Suddenly, a feeling of guilt seizes me. Why did I not rush to grab Gulla and hold him close to me? What must he think, having come all the way from remote Prang to meet me, only to be asked to stay out? Does he represent the forces that drove us out of the valley? No, that cannot be. How could I even think of that when I know for sure that he represents the bonds that held us together for centuries?

Gulla, dear Gulla of Prang, I cannot wait to meet you.

I ask the nurse to let him in. But is it too late? The spontaneity in his face and his eager demeanor, which I saw only moments earlier, has vanished. Or, is it the turbulence inside my mind that makes me think so? I come out of my chair and hold him close in a tight embrace. I offer him a seat but he stands there - the boyish face, the liquid eyes, the diffidence, the innocence exuding from every word and gesture.

"Gulla! Gulla of Prang! Oh, how changed you look! Graying already, young man? Say, how is everyone at home? How is your wife? How are the parents? Any more children? But first tell me what brings you here?" I fire questions one after another without waiting for him to answer. There is so much to ask and I am impatient to hear.

"Jenab, my heart was bursting to meet with you. I knew not where you would be. I have been enquiring everywhere all these years. Finally, a fellow villager informed me last week that you are in Jammu. I could not wait. Yesterday, I boarded the bus, reached Jammu late in the evening and passed a sleepless night in the excitement of meeting you. This is the first time ever that I have come out of Kashmir."

"I am glad you came. How is everyone?" I forget the patient in the wheelchair, and his attendant. They are looking on with open-mouthed curiosity.

I again motion him to the chair. He keeps standing.

"Jenab, time and violence took their toll. Mother passed away soon after the start of the *tehrik*. She had this fear that they may take me away."

"Oh, I am sorry to hear about your mother. But, who would take you away?"

"The army on the one hand, the militants on the other. The former taking me for a militant, the latter forcing me to join their ranks. By some providence, I escaped both."

"How is father?"

"He followed mother to the other world six months later."

"Oh, that is terrible. How is your wife?" I cannot recall her name. I feel a lump in my throat as I mutter a quick prayer for her safety.

"Jana is well, but her younger brother died in the crossfire. Many youths of the village have lost their lives, consumed by militancy, one way or the other."

"And your child? Was it a boy or a girl?"

"What child, Jenab?" He looks surprised.

I hold my breath and clench my fist so hard it pains, fearing another tragedy.

"The last we met, your wife was expecting." I ask.

"Oh, I forgot all about it. Our ill luck, Jenab; it ended in stillbirth. She had a difficult labour. We wanted to rush her to the city and get in touch with you and madam doctor, but the militants had given a call for a general strike that day. There was total paralysis of life in the valley, no vehicles were allowed on the roads. We could not leave Prang.

Curse the militancy!" He looks away like old times when he is sad.

How it must hurt him to be orphaned and childless!

"Jana never conceived again." He sighs loudly as he raises his eyes to meet mine for a fleeting moment.

I am tormented as I see the deep sadness there and realize, with intensity never felt before, what havoc terrorism has wreaked on ordinary folks in Kashmir. My own pain of displacement and exile seems to pale in front of his. I fumble for words to console him but decide to do so in a more relaxed atmosphere after I am done with the patients.

"Where did you stay the night? Go get your baggage and come here to stay with us," I urge him.

"Jenab, I have to return now. I came just to see you; the purpose of my visit has been met." He seems in a hurry.

"We have not even met properly Gulla; we have to fill in the lost years and talk a lot-about you, about Prang."

"Jenab, what is there to talk about? Everything is gone. Prang is not the same. Kashmir has changed; people have changed - there as well as here. I was fortunate to have your deedhaar again. I take your leave now. Please say my salaams to madam doctor."

"You can not leave like this, Gulla; you will come inside, meet everyone, and lunch with us," I urge him as I get up from my chair to hold him back.

He bows and departs instantly without looking back. I stand there disappointed, bewildered and, for a few moments, paralyzed like the patient waiting in the wheelchair.

10
WHAT DOES A PANDIT LOOK LIKE?

January 19, 1990 was a defining moment in the recent history of Kashmir. It was on that day that the groundswell of anti-Indian sentiment, that had been building up for some time, broke out into the open like an exploding volcano. That night, loud speakers mounted on thousands of mosques across the length and breadth of the valley, blared slogans of rebellion, and spewed out venom of intolerance against Pandits. Muslims were exhorted to come out of their homes, drive the infidels away and take on the Indian army. Pandits were threatened to join the insurgency or leave outright.

The exodus of Pandits gathered momentum after that terrifying night that still echoes in their memories. Caravans of trucks, buses and private vehicles plying on the national highway, carrying Pandits out of the valley, were a common sight. Fear and uncertainty drove them into the tempestuous seas of exile. Nobody tried to stop the exodus.

Mohan Lal, a Pandit police constable, was posted in Jammu during that upheaval. He had left his family behind in their ancestral home in Kashmir. Since police personnel were special targets of the militants, Mohan Lal did not think it prudent to travel to Srinagar and bring his family out. He asked his wife to stay on until he arranged their safe passage to Jammu.

The family lived in Motiyar at Rainawari. Raina is a common surname among Pandits, Rainawari literally meaning the abode of Rainas. It was a predominantly Hindu enclave of the city, and a strikingly snug place along the backwaters of Dal Lake that gave it a pastoral ambience. Shalimar, Nishat, and the floating gardens were within rowing distances. Dainty Shikaras, laden with fresh vegetables and fruit, glided past many houses along the backwaters, and quacking ducks sailed elegantly and dived headlong into the water to forage for food. Tightly built compact houses with facades of delicate narrow maharaji bricks, latticed woodwork and large balconies, stood in neat rows on narrow lanes.

Most homes had vegetable patches. This pretty enclave was now fast getting depleted of its Pandit population. Within a few weeks there were hardly any Pandit households left in Motiyar where Mohan Lal's family had lived for generations.

Mohan Lal's wife, Sheela, waited anxiously for him to arrange for their evacuation. One evening, she received a phone call from a stranger. In a gruff and menacing voice the caller asked her why she was still around when all the *kafirs* had run away. He warned her that she was being watched, accused her of spying and passing on information to her husband, and threatened her with dire consequences. The phone slipped from her hand as she trembled with fear and started crying. Her children, Amit and Shivani, clung to her and shouted for grandmother Chaanda.

Chaanda was a boisterous woman, whose lewd jokes made many a damsel blush. People loved her for her warmth and openness. In a land where few women ventured to swim in public, she had mastered the duck stroke that made it possible for her to swim without exposing her body. She often jumped into the water for a cool dip on a hot summer day or after an argument with her husband. She was brave, and had kept her poise when militants had barged into a Pandit house close by, shot a young man and walked away with impunity. She believed no one would harm her family because of her closeness to Muslim friends and neighbors. But the intimidating phone call to her daughter-in-law made her cower with fear. For the first time in her life, she felt terribly insecure.

Chaanda decided that they should leave at the earliest opportunity and join her son in Jammu. They would not inform him because his life could be in danger if he decided to come home and accompany them out to safety. In Rainawari, it was easy for the militants to strike at will and then disappear in the narrow lanes, jump over mud fences, and make their escape through the backwaters.

Fearing the worst, the family spent the night in great distress. There was no time to pack and take their belongings along. At daybreak, they bolted the windows and doors, locked their house and left the keys with their neighbour Mohammad Syed. He was a family friend and a bulwark of support in these difficult times. He wished so much to stop them from leaving but feared for them and for himself. Times were bad. You could not afford to be seen helping or sympathizing with Pandits; sheltering them or persuading them to stay back was out of the question. Your own colleagues and friends, even your children, might inform on you. Many concerned Muslims asked their Pandit friends to get out of the valley, for some time, to escape the mayhem and madness that had gripped the place.

***

After the departure of Mohan Lal's family, Mohammed Syed's young daughters, Ruhi Jan and Sabiya, who often played with his children of about the same age, were disconsolate. They missed them for weeks on end and kept asking questions that made their parents uncomfortable. The Pandits that left the valley had expected to return soon, with the sanguine hope that the security forces would crush the militancy in a matter of months if not weeks. But far from eradicating it, even containing the militancy turned out to be a long drawn out process. Slowly, the Pandits, tired of waiting for normalcy to return in their homeland, struck roots in places that they had sought as temporary refuges in exile.

Mohammad Syed would often get nostalgic about the Pandits when the family sat together and reminisced about old times. He rued the fact that strange people had come to live in Motiyar, some of them unsavory and uncultured-boatmen, who had spent their life on the water in shabby *doongas* fighting verbal battles and heaping abuse on each other for hours on end and carrying the fight to the next day, and the next. He missed Pandits who were generally friendly, even docile. His nostalgia puzzled his daughters who found this at variance with what they learnt about Pandits from friends and teachers in their school-that they were selfish and greedy, double—faced, never to be trusted. They heard stories of their treachery, of how they hated

Muslims, opposed *Azadi* and acted as spies and informers. Pandits slowly took shape as monsters in the minds of the new generation of Muslim children in Kashmir.

***

"What does a Pandit look like?" Sabiya, nine years old by now, asked her mother.

"Well, they look like us. Why do you ask?"

"Because they are different, aren't they? They dress and speak and pray differently. They are not good people."

"That is not so. You should not be talking like this," mother admonished her.

"But that is what every one tells us," insisted Sabiya.

"Yes, they are ogle-eyed, horn-headed, elephant-eared, seven-fingered, snub-nosed…," Mohammad Syed butted in jokingly, amused at the expression of disbelief in the eyes of his daughters.

"My friend said that Mallakhah is overflowing with the dead because of the treachery of Pandits. Now, there is no more burial ground left," Ruhi Jan put in.

"Girls, this is utter nonsense; how can you believe this rubbish?" Mohammad Syed rebuked his daughters. "The Pandits are no different from us. Mohan Lal was our best friend. I have not met a better person in all my life."

But, the girls were not convinced and the picture painted by others outside their home remained etched in their minds and in the minds of their friends.

***

Mohammad Syed did his best to guard Mohan Lal's house as a sacred trust. He retrieved his important documents, jewellery shawls and saris from their steel closet soon after their escape and took them personally to Jammu to hand them over to his friend. He managed to keep trespassers at bay for some time but could not stop the tide of vandals who looted, bit by bit, what remained in the house. A militant group seized control of the house against his protestations and used it for several months, until the soldiers flushed them out during a search operation. Some time later, a family moved in and stayed on. It was jungle law and people like the Syeds felt out of place. He watched mutely, the breakdown of social order and despaired.

Mohan Lal could do nothing from Jammu to undo the illegal occupation of his house, even though he was in the police department. Police had lost all credibility and control. Hardly anyone ventured to return and reclaim their homes. Neither did Mohan Lal. He consoled himself that he was not alone in this tragedy. In fact, he was lucky that his house had not been torched like hundreds of Pandit houses, and it gave him some satisfaction that it was providing warmth and comfort to some people, even though they were unknown to him and paid him no rent.

***

Years went by. Ruhi Jan, a high school student now, came down with a strange affliction. She started losing interest in studies and performed poorly. She became sullen and suspicious, avoiding crowds and friends. An obsession for cleanliness possessed her, of washing her hands repeatedly and spending hours in the bath room. She was reluctant to eat anything. She lost weight and the pink of her cheeks. Her parents took her to several doctors in Srinagar but she continued to withdraw from her friends and family and preferred the solitude of her room. Her parents despaired and did not know whom to turn to. A family friend suggested that they contact a doctor in Jammu. Mohammad Syed was sceptical. Travelling to Jammu would cause a major upheaval in the family. He would have to find a suitable place to live. The girls had never gone anywhere outside the valley. They had not seen a Pandit in flesh and blood since the mass exodus of the community. Now Ruhi was to be treated by a Pandit doctor. How would she take it?

Mohammad Syed took his family into confidence. "How about a winter holiday in Jammu, girls?" he asked. "Your school is closed for winter and you deserve a break. It will be a good change and a reprieve from the severe cold here. Besides, I hear there is a well-known Kashmiri doctor in Jammu. Let us see if he can help Ruhi."

Every one grabbed at the suggestion. Yes, they deserved a change. It would be good to get away for a while from the skirmishes, the strikes and the general insecurity that had become a feature of daily life in Kashmir.

Mohammad Syed thought of Mohan Lal and phoned him.

Mohan Lal jumped with excitement: "What a coincidence that I happen to personally know the doctor you want to consult. I hope I will be able to get an early appointment for Ruhi Jan. The schools must have closed for the winter break in Kashmir. This is the ideal time for your family to visit Jammu and renew old ties with my family."

Mohammad Syed was delighted. He asked Mohan Lal to rent a suitable place for them. They would spend a few weeks in Jammu and combine Ruhi Jan's treatment with a holiday. This would also be a chance to meet old Pandit friends who were now living in Jammu.

For Mohan Lal this was an opportunity to return the favours of his erstwhile neighbour—in the words of his mother, 'to discharge the debt of friendship'. He lived in a small flat allotted to him by his department. The Syeds would stay with him, he decided. He vacated a room to keep it at the disposal of the Syeds, and installed a gas stove and cooking paraphernalia for use by them during their stay.

Mohammad Syed, his wife, and daughters were overwhelmed by the welcome. For dinner, Sheela had spent considerable time cooking dishes she knew her guests liked. Mother Chaanda had grown quite old but she had not lost her sense of humour. She was affectionate as usual and regaled them with the tales of her youth in Motiyar and the travails in Jammu. Son Amit was away in Pune, pursuing his engineering but Shivani was in town, completing her high school. She was soft spoken and coy, but could not speak Kashmiri fluently. The girls took to each other easily. By the second day, they settled down to a comfortable routine and on the third, Mohan Lal accompanied Ruhi Jan and her father to the doctor.

Ruhi Jan had frequent consultations with the doctor, who encouraged the whole family to join in the sessions. She was put on medication and the doctor suggested family outings to various places in Jammu that might distract Ruhi Jan from her compulsive thoughts and obsessions.

Mohan Lal arranged tours for the guests to the wild life sanctuary at Manda, the Bahu Fort, Pir Bhaba and Chenab. Shivani spent time in the evenings with them after she returned from college. The girls shared their experiences, their fears and hopes. Sheela accompanied them to shopping in the famous Raghunath Bazar. It was a new experience for the guests from Kashmir.

The Syed girls wondered what terrible lies had they been told about Pandits. Why had they refused to believe their own father who often spoke highly of them? Was it possible this happened to be an exceptional Pandit family that did not fit in with the sordid picture they had created in their minds from hearsay? But they found several other Pandits who came visiting Mohan Lal's home equally warm and friendly.

"You were right Daddy; we had been so ill informed about the Pandits. They are like us in every way; they eat like us, think like us and talk our language. Besides, they are so kind and considerate," Sabiya told her father.

"Why did they have to leave Kashmir?" Ruhi Jan asked.

"I am delighted that you have changed your opinion about Pandits. Let us hope things will improve and our Pandit friends will return home in the near future."

***

Before long, Ruhi Jan showed signs of improvement. Her obsessions became less pervasive, her appetite improved, the melancholia wore off and her old gregariousness began to reassert itself. The family spent a month and a half in Jammu, by which time she was on the road to recovery. The warmth shown by their hosts, and the warm weather warmed their souls. For the girls it was an experience they would never forget.

The parting was emotional. The Syeds could not thank their hosts enough. They invited them to Kashmir. Militancy was dying down and there was no need to be afraid, Mohammad Syed assured them.

"But what is left for us there? There are no Pandits out there.

Our houses have been vandalized, torched or occupied; our jobs and business have been taken over; our temples are in ruin. Besides, you do not want us there," Chaanda could not restrain herself.

"Let me assure you mother, we want you back. We are fond of Pandits and feel incomplete without them. I hope we can make amends," Mohammad Syed said with genuine feeling. "You can live with us till you move into your own house. You know it still stands."

"But you said a family lives there?" Mohan Lal asked.

"Yes, a family does live in your house, but it is your home and you can have them thrown out if they do not vacate it voluntarily. We can take help from the District Commissioner who is supposed to be the custodian of Pandit properties. Times have changed. You must visit Kashmir to see for yourself," Mohammad Syed reassured him as he boarded the bus to Kashmir.

Mohan Lal promised to visit them at the earliest opportunity.

***

While the Jammu visit of the Syeds was providential, the opportunity to fulfill his promise of a return visit to Kashmir came soon after for Mohan Lal when he was promoted as an inspector and deputed for a weeklong official visit to Srinagar. He would normally have resisted going there on one pretext or another, but it was tempting to see his old home, and find out for himself how Kashmir had changed during the last seventeen years. He seized the opportunity and took the bus to Srinagar.

On arrival, he was put up in a hotel in uptown Srinagar. He phoned his friend soon after he checked in. Mohammad Syed invited him to lunch the following Sunday.

Mohan Lal took the official jeep to Rainawari, asked the driver to park at Jogilanker near the police station and started on foot to the Syed residence.

It was a strange experience to walk the lanes of Motiyar after so many years. The place was unrecognizable and he felt like an alien. New homes had sprouted everywhere. Some Pandit houses had been redone with a modern makeover, others were in utter disrepair and unrecognizable, yet others had been burnt down or reduced to rubble. Unfamiliar faces looked out from the windows of the houses, the owners of which he would have known by first names in days gone by. Some of them smiled and others looked curiously at him. Yes, he was a stranger here. This was not the Rainawari he knew and grew up in.

***

Mohan Lal was received with great warmth by the Syed family. They had prepared Kashmiri food in the wazawan style—several courses of lamb, chicken, and saffron rice. Several family friends of the Syeds had also been invited. There was a lot of bonhomie and talk about the old times and the prevailing conditions in Srinagar.

While the party was on, children from the neighbourhood started trickling into the Syed courtyard, soon to swell into a crowd. Word had gone round that a Pandit was visiting the Syeds. The children were eager to see what a Pandit looked like. There were whispers, murmurs, chuckles and loud laughter as the kids jostled and clamoured for vantage positions near the window to get a look inside the room where Mohan Lal was enjoying a cup of *kehva*, that followed the meal. The children craned their necks to look in from the windowpanes, their faces burning with curiosity to catch a glimpse of this alien!

"Which one, which one?" they asked each other, pointing their little fingers at the assembly inside.

There was commotion as a child fell down trying to climb on the back of another to have a good look at Mohan Lal. It drew the attention of the people inside. They looked in disbelief at this riot of children outside trying to peep in. Mohammad Syed came out of the house. This was the first time he had so many visitors. He recognized some of them; there were others he had never seen before.

"What are you all here for, may I know?" He addressed the crowd.

The children kept looking at him and at each other. They had heard all kinds of stories about Pandits and wondered why the Syeds should have invited one to their home. Now was the chance to actually see one. The irrepressible kids were in no mood to leave until their curiosity was satisfied.

After a long pause a little kid suddenly blurted out, "We want to see what a Pandit looks like."

When Mohan Lal came to learn that he was the focus of this great *tamasha*, he burst out in loud laughter that startled every one, and came out to face the motley crowd with curious expressions on their charming faces.

"Can the children come in; I want to say a few words to them?" he asked his hosts.

Before the hosts could say yes, the kids rushed inside, each trying to sit as close to him as possible. Soon, the room was overflowing with children and echoing with their chatter.

Mohan Lal had walked to the other end of the room and seated himself on a table to face them. He was broad shouldered, of medium height, with straight hair parted left of centre. He sported a small moustache and a wide smile.

"Children, I am told that you have come here to see me, to know about me. Well, that is flattering, for I do not remember an occasion when so many people were interested in me."

"He is not a monster; he looks like Bashir Sahib, our Urdu teacher," one of the kids shouted. There was loud laughter.

"I see, you are all eager to know what a Kashmiri Pandit looks like," Mohan Lal continued.

"I do not see any horns on his head," another kid shouted. The hosts felt embarrassed but Mohan Lal laughed again, louder than before.

"Well, look carefully at me," he resumed. "My name is Mohan Lal Safaya and I am a Kashmiri Pandit. I have eyes and ears like you, I speak the same language as you, eat the same food as you, think like you, dream like you. I have children who are like you. In fact, it feels like you all are my own children. Motiyar was my home. I lived here with my wife, mother and two children in that house, over there. That was our small beautiful world."

As he pointed at his house across the lane, he stopped suddenly, took a deep sigh and started sobbing loudly. His face was contorted with emotion and he started crying like a child, stunning the whole gathering of children and adults alike into dead silence. Mohammad Syed and other adults rose to comfort him. The women who had now gathered wiped their tearful eyes. There was general sighing, sobbing and sniffing in the hall.

Then a miracle happened. A child rose, walked towards Mohan

Lal, shook his hands, and kept shaking it for quite some time, proudly smiling at the assembly. There was spontaneous applause and the sobbing gave way to loud laughter and bonhomie. Other kids rose one by one to touch Mohan Lal and shake his hand, as if wanting to reassure themselves. There was joy on their faces. The transformation seemed electric, magical.

Kashmiris are songsters who give vent to expressions that match the intensity of their emotions. By now, the neighbourhood adults had also poured into the Syed home. The assembled women took no time in threading together a Vanvun and sang in chorus:

Do you know, Mohan Lal is back with us here?

Do you know, a son has returned to his mother?

Pray, who cast his evil eye on Kashmir?

Pray, who estranged fond brothers from each other?

Have we not suffered more than our share?

Isn't it time a brother reunites with a brother?

Do you know how sorely we miss the Pandits?

Do you know how incomplete we feel in Kashmir?

Can there be a garden with a single-hued flower

When diversity is the very basis of Nature?

Do you know, Mohan Lal is back in Motiyar?

Do you know, a son has returned to his mother?

The strains of the Vanvun seemed to float on the summer breeze and evoked memories of his past life in Rainawari - the sounds and smells, the springs and the snows, the lakes and the shikaras, the temples and the mosques, the Shivratris and the Eids - as Mohan Lal listened, his eyes moist with emotion. By the time the Vanvun was over, he wore an ecstatic look on his face.

Soon, it was time to leave.

"Come and pay us a visit in Jammu and I will show you around, and introduce you to Pandit children. I am sure they will want to be friends with you," Mohan Lal addressed the kids as he rose to bid adieu. They looked at him with expressions that were a mix of wonder, warmth and admiration. They kept sitting there, not wanting this encounter to end.

Mohammad Syed asked, "Don't you want to see your house before you leave?"

Mohan Lal hesitated for a while, unsure, but his host pressed on, "There should be no problem. Let us go and have a look. After all, it is your own home. Chandaa and Sheela will be dying to know about it on your return."

They walked across the lane to his house. The mud walls around his garden patch had been redone in brick. The house had not changed. Intertwining vines of cucumber and gourd rose up from the ground to the balcony on the second floor. The front window of the balcony, from where Mohan Lal would enjoy the view of the snowcapped mountains in the distance, was closed. He was now near the outer door, about to knock, when a window opened from the first-floor bedroom. A middle-aged couple looked out and smiled genially at him, the curious smile proud homeowners would give to a casual passer by. There was no guilt, no fear, and no hostility in their expression. Mohan Lal froze for a while, smiled back at them, and moved on as if he never intended to knock or enter. Mohammad Syed was surprised. Before he could speak, Mohan Lal pre-empted him and asked, "Can we take a walk; I want to look around Rainawari?"

They walked on. Mohan Lal avoided answering his friend

as to why he did not step inside his house. It was a warm sunny afternoon. He enjoyed walking the narrow lanes he had frequented in his childhood. He wanted to take in the whole scene—the back waters, the floating gardens, the mountain ranges and the snow peaks, the Hari Parbat fort right in the middle of the city and the Shankaracharya temple shinning atop another hill—landmarks that no militancy could possibly erase. He remembered how on Sunday mornings, when they were young, Mohammad Syed and he would walk all the way to Hari Parbat. He would visit the Ganesha temple while his friend would climb the stairs to Makhdoom Sahib's shrine nearby. They would return home by noon.

They walked on and on. The sun started going down behind the hills, magically transforming the landscape, as the clouds clinging to the mountains assumed different shapes and hues that changed fast. Mohan Lal took a deep breath as if to take in everything of this ambience so he would retain the memory of this day for the rest of his life. His eyes swept the scene from east to west and north to south and then he turned to his friend, "Let us return, the driver must be waiting."

"What about the visit to your house? Don't you want to go in and tell the people there that they will have to vacate it soon?" Mohammad Syed asked.

"I don't think I will. Seventeen years is a long time, my friend. A lot has changed. Spaces that we left behind have been filled. Displacement can be terrible for anyone. I know it. I have experienced it," Mohan Lal replied after a long pause.

11
THE FISH OF MATTAN

On a cold and foggy January morning, Gouri Koul was wheeled into my clinic by her grandson Sanjay and granddaughter Achilla. She gave me a look of recognition with a wide smile.

Extending her cold, quivering and stiff right hand towards me, she said, "You saved my life five years back; you have to do it again."

She seemed quite animated to meet me and did not appear to be in any major distress. It would have hurt her to know that I did not remember her. Possibly, Sanjay understood my predicament. He promptly produced the case file I had logged during her previous visits. It was all there: She had consulted me five years earlier for a stroke that had caused paralysis of her right side and a speech disability. She had improved appreciably during the four weeks she had been under my care. By then, she could lift her arm but was unable to perform fine movements; she could move her leg but could not walk unaided; her speech had become intelligible but she was left with some loss of fluency.

"I did not see you all these years?" I asked her.

"I was back in Mattan and never felt the need to come here. I followed your instructions and have vastly improved since I saw you," she replied.

"What brings you here now?"

"I was reasonably well until last week when I had a nosebleed. It was a stream that did not stop for fifteen minutes and scared me so much I thought my end was near. Finally, they poured cold water on my head, pinched my nose and stuffed it with cotton wool. Fortunately the bleeding stopped but I am scared it might happen again. I could not wait to see you. I trust you will take care of me."

"Do you still live in Mattan? How many Pandits are left there?" I was curious to know.

Sanjay responded to my query. "She never left the place. There used to be nearly five hundred families. Now there are seven. All others fled in the 1990 exodus."

Gouri was pretty and petite at seventy two. She wore the traditional tweed pheron. A woollen scarf covered her head and neck . It made her look like a little girl. She had adjusted so well to her disability that she did not complain about it. She did not ask me why she had not recovered enough to not need help. She had reconciled to the handicap, possibly even forgotten that she had ever been normal.

I examined her in detail. Her right wrist and elbow were stiff. She walked with help and could barely raise her right arm which was held close to her body, flexed at the elbow and slightly dropped at the wrist. She had developed a frozen shoulder. Her blood pressure was elevated.

I wrote a prescription.

"I think your high blood pressure might have caused the nose bleed. The pills should help bring it down. You need to exercise your limbs to relax the joints," I advised her.

"Can I return home?" she asked.

"I hear it is quite cold in Kashmir. It has snowed heavily this year and the Dal Lake is freezing. It will do you good to spend another month in Jammu. What is the hurry?" I asked.

"Because the fish will be waiting," she replied in earnest.

I got curious; she seemed to be talking in parables.

"What fish?" I asked

"The fish in the Mattan spring."

It was getting really interesting.

"Waiting for what?" I asked.

"Waiting for their feed". She spoke as if it was normal for fish to wait for a person.

"But you are barely able to walk, even with help. How do you get to the spring to feed the fish? How do you negotiate the terraces and the steps? How far is your home from the spring?"

"I have not visited the spring since I was struck with paralysis though it is just a few hundred meters from my home. Achilla takes the feed to the fish everyday," she said, looking towards her grand daughter with pride.

"Have you made any arrangements for the fish during your absence, now that Achilla is here with you? I asked her.

"How could I leave home if I had not taken care of that? I left the feed with the neighbours," she replied with a sense of satisfaction.

I looked at Achilla. She smiled and nodded in approval.

"You did not leave Kashmir, Achilla?" I asked.

"No sir, I stayed behind with my grandmother."

"What do you do besides feeding the fish?" I asked jokingly.

Rosy faced, with hair combed back and plaited into a long pony tail, Achilla, the daughter of Gouri's son, smiled and said she was an arts graduate waiting for a teacher's job.

"Where did you graduate from?" I asked.

"From the Women's college, Srinagar."

"How did you manage to do that if you lived in Mattan with your grandmother? It is such a large distance to Srinagar," I asked surprised.

"I commuted everyday."

"That must not have been easy in such trying times."

"It was challenging."

"Was there any other Pandit girl in your class?"

"No sir, I was the only one."

"Was it safe? Where you not frightened to be the only Pandit girl around?"

"There was no choice."

"Did you feel vulnerable?"

"In a way, yes, but I had to think about my studies." She was forthright in her replies.

Turning again to Sanjay, I asked, "Why do the fish need your feed? There is enough in the spring that nature provides. In fact, you should not feed the fish. They thrive better on the natural food available in the spring."

"This is not the usual fish that you see in rivers, lakes and springs. The fish of Mattan spring are special. They wait for their feed. You have to go and visit them to see for yourself; how they swim to the surface and look at you when you go near. If you walk slowly along the spring, they follow you in swarms."

I was reminded of the beautiful spring of Mattan. My first visit to the town was several decades back, when my grandfather was the headmaster of the Mattan High School and I was eight. I spent two weeks there. We would visit the temple and watch the fish for hours and feed them rice flakes. I had watched the spectacle of the fish following the visitors who came with packets of food for them. In later years, on way to Pahalgam where we often spent a large portion of our summer break, we would visit the famous Mattan temple and watch the fabulous fish in the shimmering spring.

"They follow you like beggars because you have given them a bad habit. They do not need to strive for food when it comes so easy. They have become fat and lazy because of your pampering; they have fallen into bad habits."

"Please sir, do not speak disparagingly about our fish. We are already cursed. Do not bring more curses upon us," Sanjay protested.

"I seem to have hurt your sentiments," I said, "but I have no reason to believe that the fish of Mattan are different from any other fish in the world. How is it that you believe in the sacredness of a spring or the fish that reside there?" I was trying to probe rather than provoke him.

Handsome, with smiling eyes and abundant confidence, Sanjay was a career councilor at Jammu. He was the son of Gouri's daughter. That family had also fled Kashmir during the exodus of 1990. He grew up and studied in Jammu but paid regular visits to Mattan to see his grandmother.

"Doctor Sahib, there is no doubt about the sacredness of the Mattan temple and the spring there. In fact, there were enough warning signs that preceded the bad times in Kashmir. But we never paid any heed till we were overwhelmed by the cataclysmic events that brought misfortune upon every one," he spoke with conviction.

Coming from an educated, modern looking young man, I proceeded to explore the basis of such strong faith.

"Pray, what were the signs?" I asked.

"It all started with the felling of the Bren tree."

"Where was the tree? Who felled it?"

"The big Bren in the Mattan temple yard. The management decided to cut the tree down. They planned to construct a dharamshala at that spot. We tried to dissuade them from this sacrilege, but they would not relent. The tree came down with a big crash and the earth shook. From the trunk gushed a stream of blood like from the neck of a slaughtered sheep. Blood continued to ooze from the fallen trunk and the stump for several hours. The tree was weeping tears of blood. We were sad and frightened and knew something terrible was going to happen. The curse had fallen; the first killing of Pandits started soon after."

This was proving to be an extraordinary tale. Yet there had to be a rational explanation.

"It must have been the sap. There are other trees also with red sap-red maple and redwoods, for example," I explained.

"You are right, sir. Red blood runs in our veins and red sap flows in the veins of the trees. What is the difference? It is the same life force in both."

I was impressed by his interpretation.

"It was very painful to see the red fluid oozing from the tree that evening. It was an ancient tree, as sacred as the spring itself. We used to worship the tree as we worship the spring. We should not have cut it down."

"Yes, we must try to preserve trees. They are our heritage, especially the Bren and the Chinar. But the rate at which we have been cutting down trees and building in and around our temple premises, we are not only destroying the landscape but also the sanctity and the serenity of these places of worship," I lamented. "However, we should not fall victim to superstition. That is even worse," I added.

"Sir, it is not superstition but a firm belief I am speaking from. Militancy struck Kashmir soon after that event. It was the curse from the devta who resided in the Bren."

"There is a devta in each one of us, in our trees and even our homes. That is the spirit, the life force you speak about. However, do you think the cutting down of one tree would have brought such misery upon the people of Kashmir?"

"That was certainly one of the reasons, howsoever minor. There were other curses because of the bad ways society had fallen into. We reaped the harvest of the cumulative sins of the community," he concluded.

The young man could not be faulted for his moral rectitude. I decided to change the subject before I inadvertently hurt him by some unsavoury remarks.

"There used to be red fish in the spring?" I enquired. "I remember seeing them in my childhood. People claimed that they were special to the Mattan spring."

"Yes, there was one red fish, but it disappeared. That happened nearly three months after the tree was felled."

"How does one explain its disappearance?" I asked.

"The red fish was a manifestation of the spring deity. It would give audience in the mornings and, sometimes, in the evenings. It never failed the devotees."

"Do you really believe so?"

"Certainly," he replied, "it was an incarnation. Like matsya avatar, the fish incarnation of Vishnu."

"Why in your opinion did it stop appearing?"

"As a warning of the bad times, the cataclysms to come," he replied as if that was the most logical explanation.

Strangely, I developed a liking for this broad cheeked, red-faced, genial and unpretentious young man.

"Someone may have stolen it. It could be mischief, an attempt to intimidate the Pandits, to disenchant them of their faith," I said for want of any other explanation.

"No one would dare to commit such a sacrilege. Even the local Muslims hold the spring in reverence and the fish sacred. You might know the famous Kashmiri adage: The spring fish is a blessing to watch and a sin to catch. That is what both the Hindus and Muslims believe."

"But the militants have no morals, no religion, except what has been drilled into their heads."

"No one can catch the red fish. It is just not possible. How can one harm the divine?"

I had no answer to Sanjay's entrenched beliefs.

"There was yet another ominous sign," Sanjay went on. "The colour of the spring would never change in normal times. It was always sparkling and you could see the bottom of the spring, fair weather or foul. Rain, snow and sleet would never change its colour.

But that year, the spring turned muddy for the first time for no reason whatsoever. All these things can not be explained away as a series of mere coincidences. They were clear signs that we unfortunately failed to recognize."

"What could you have done anyway? It was not in your hands to stop the terror and mayhem the militants let loose. All you could have done was to run away and save your lives. You did that; we all did that."

He nodded his head thoughtfully.

"Why did your family stay back in the face of such danger?" I asked Achilla.

"When nearly all the Pandits left, the fish started disappearing from the spring."

"Did they?" I asked in wonder.

"Yes, they swam downstream, following the fleeing Pandits, begging them to return. It was a strange sight. The fish must have felt the pain of the Pandits leaving their homes and hearths."

"Or, because they lost their source of sustenance?" I laughed.

She nodded uncertainly.

"Because, they had gotten used to easy pickings," I gently taunted her. "Can you tell me how many of the five hundred Pandit families would feed the fish?"

"Nearly all. They came with rice, teher, bread, grains, and almost everything we eat."

"Except salt," put in Gouri.

"That is why the spring would abound with them and you saw shoals of fish that you could catch with your bare hands, if you so desired," I continued. "When the Pandits left, the fish started to starve, and they left the spring and went downstream till there were only a few left."

It was Sanjay who continued the thread of the conversation. "That may be an explanation, sir. In any case, what is a spring worth without fish? When we witnessed the exodus of the fish, grandmother said she would stay back, come what may. She was perfectly healthy then and would never fail to pray in the temple and feed the fish every morning. Even my father decided to leave because there was a threat to his life, for being an employee of the police department. Seven more families decided to stay back after grandmother's decision. They may have had their own reasons, but I am sure the fish were on their minds as well.

"Do they regret the decision?"

"I do not think so. Certainly, not my grandmother. And I am happy for her. Her soul resides in Mattan - the temple and the spring and the fish."

"Are the fish back?"

"Yes, we picked bushels of fish from downstream and put them back in the spring and started feeding them again. We appealed to the local administration for more provisions because we could not afford all the needs of the fish. The assistant commissioner issued an order to the ration depot granting a regular ration for the fish. Now we have the spring back in its pristine glory."

"Except the red fish that never returned," Gouri drew a long sigh.

"What could be the reason?" I asked.

"It is a sign of the changed milieu of Kashmir. The red fish is angry and has gone into hiding. Who knows, it may reappear in better times?" she replied with a sigh.

"It may be waiting for the Pandits to return," I uttered instinctively. There was no sarcasm in my statement.

"Possibly," she drew another long sigh.

"If the migration of fish could be reversed, why not the exodus of the Pandits? It requires a strong will from the administration," Sanjay said.

"And the will of the Pandits," I added.

"Exactly!" Sanjay was excited to hear me say it. "I hope the day is not far when we will have everyone back."

With a strange light in her eyes, Gouri made an invocation in her quivering voice, "Tathaastu."

"Tathaastu," I repeated.

"Tathaastu," Sanjay and Achilla echoed together.

12

TRUCE

She was big, black and crafty. Whenever I caught her on the prowl in my garden, she eyed me with suspicion and hostility. I would not mind her trespass, had it not been for her audacity and for what transpired in the days to come.

I started hearing distress calls from the birds in my garden that distracted me from my work and woke me up from my midday naps. I would rush outside and find her lazily passing by, in utter disdain of the birds that hollered at her to keep her away from their little ones in the nests. They flew from one tree to another to give her chase, daring her, beating about their wings, hovering over her, raising the pitch of their cacophony and clamour–alas, with little impact. I threatened her with my fist and scowled at her, but she remained unfazed and kept looking at me, indifferently, till she watched me pick a pebble. She bolted away before I threw it at her, disappearing in the bushes, only to emerge a while later to climb over the wall and scamper across to the neighbour's.

In course of time I began to discover pieces of bird wings and feathers in the far corners of my lawn and realized that she had gobbled up some of the little ones. Leela, my wife, would get upset. She loved her winged friends, adored watching their frolic and listening to their orchestra. She filled pans and pots of all descriptions with fresh water every morning, for the birds to enjoy a drink and have a bath. She replenished the plates regularly with leftovers that the birds relished so much. On birthdays and other auspicious occasions, she cooked the traditional yellow rice and fed it to them before serving the family. Mother too revelled in similar indulgences. She would not break her fast until she had torn a large chunk off her flatbread, broken it into small pieces with her skinny fingers, and handed it over to me or Leela to feed the birds. She would never forget to inquire if we had served the first handful of boiled rice to them before we started our lunch. I would often joke that the birds were getting fat and lazy from our ministrations.

The discovery of bird remains in the garden annoyed and saddened us. More so, because we had watched the whole process from the nesting on the orange trees outside our bedroom window, to the laying of the eggs, to the birth of squeaking hatchlings with open beaks, ready for the morsels their parents took turns to fetch, without respite, to feed their voracious appetites.

We had to go on the offensive to keep the marauding cat at bay. Leela kept a pile of pebbles handy. At the earliest call of birds in distress, she ran out with a handful to throw at this felon. She never succeeded in hitting the target. Nor did I. The missiles would invariably fall wide off the mark. Hurling pebbles at her was no remedy, we realized soon enough. Sometimes, I only managed to pull an arm muscle in doing so. Running after the cat left me breathless and the cat curious. I had a feeling she was amused at my antics. I gave up chasing her and thought of trying to aim sling shots at her. I spent precious hours on target practice. But when it came to our adversary, I realized how difficult it was to hit a moving feline.

We thought of other strategies to keep the cat away. Keeping a dog was an option but that had its own problems - the additional responsibility of looking after it. Raising the fence higher was another option but the cat would climb any height without much effort and squeeze her way through any thistle with ease. The higher we raised the fence the more did her curiosity grow, and more the urgency to jump inside. If curiosity ever killed a cat, I was not a witness to it.

The butchery went on as we discovered more and more feathers and limbs. Leela was angry. I tried to remind her of the laws of survival - large fish eating small fish, birds helping themselves to worms, cats preying on rats and hatchlings, and humans gorging on everything from vegetables to fruits, pigeons to prawns, fish to fowl.

I argued: "What about the hoopoe who pirouettes around our lawn, tirelessly digging the earth for worms? How fondly we watch and admire it digging the worm out with that long curved beak, raising his crest in pride, and moving to a distant corner to enjoy its delicious meal. That is our earthworm he eats, the worm that turns our soil to give it air. Why does that not cause us pain? 'The early bird catches the worm,' we quote so matter-of-factly without ever thinking of the cruelty of it."

But, Leela was inconsolable, and slapped an emphatic reply: "Why should this sly creature invade our premises to eat our birds when there is the whole big world out there for her to roam about and hunt? Besides, she violates nature's law because she does not catch what she is supposed to-the mice that are scampering all round us here. But, that takes some running and chasing, and she is so lazy she does not bother, having grown fat and flabby feeding on our birds. We have to get rid of her somehow."

An internet search on how to keep a cat at bay did not make us any wiser. And while I sought advice from other knowledgeable sources, something worse happened. As if in retaliation to our intimidation and scheming to keep her away, she started defecating on the front porch of our outhouse, where I examine my patients. Every morning, I would shudder as I approached the porch to find the shit. A cat crossing your path is an omen bad enough, but to catch the sight of a cat and, worse still, its excrement, first thing in the morning, is too much to bear. Yet, there was no way out except to hold one's breath, scoop it up and hurl it into a far corner of the garden behind the bushes. Often, I had to sweep and wash the floor and dry it with a mop before I opened the door for the patients waiting outside. It became a daily chore except when she gave me a reprieve, and a false hope that she had taken pity on me by virtue of some cat sense, only to discover that she had duped me again. Once, I hid behind the drapes of my consulting chamber in a bid to catch her red-handed and punish her somehow for her misdemeanor. But she was too cunning and managed to skip my vigil, to leave behind yet another evidence of her misdeed.

We were still debating and devising schemes to fight this menace when there was a new development. We started hearing raucous noises during the night. We wondered for a few days about this nightly disturbance to finally discover another feline on the scene, a suitor who must have sniffed the cat and trailed her to her haunts in our garden. A heady courtship ensued over the following days and we tried to sleep over it. But the flimsy mantle of peace was soon torn apart with the appearance of new sounds, now of a multitude of cats who threw themselves into the ring - tails, heads, whiskers and all. Little skirmishes led to fierce battles, breaking the silence of the night. There could be no truce; the battles had to be fought to the very end until many a suitor was vanquished and forced to withdraw with his tails tucked tightly between hind legs, and retreat in favour of a huge brown tomcat who now laid the sole claim to our black tormentor.

By a strange coincidence the nightly defilement stopped, and thankfully, the daily cleaning ritual came to an end as the courtship grew and we graciously resigned ourselves to their amorous escapades within our precincts.

But, as with humans, the heady days of romance were over before we realized it. Curiously, we no longer saw the brown visitor, and it soon became clear he was done with the romancing since his paramour had grown thoughtful, moody and heavy. Ah, the faithless lover!

And then, I heard strangely pleading and poignant sounds during the middle of a night which seemed to come from near our bedroom window, as if a female was in pain. I got up to find out if someone had jumped over the fence along with a sick patient that needed my urgent attention. I came out but found nobody. Was it a dream? I went back to sleep only to be woken up again by that distressful call. I could now, not mistake it for anything except a cat. What was she crying about, I wondered? Could she be in labour, now that we had observed the unmistakable signs? Could she know Leela was an obstetrician! Nevertheless, I would not wake her up for this adversary who had tormented us all along. I dug my head into the pillow and wished her away.

Come next morning, and I had forgotten the nocturnal episode. A few days later, I heard a curiously pleasing sound coming from the distant corner of our lawn. There was no doubt it was the mewing of kittens from behind the bushes. I walked across to find out. As soon as I parted the bushes to get closer, the familiar black cat jumped out and climbed the wall, perching on it, looking beseechingly at me. I looked inside the bush but found nothing. I looked inside an empty drum nearby, that had been left on the refuse dump behind the bushes, and it was here that I saw a litter of lovely little kittens – black brown triplets, true to the genes they had inherited - looking up innocently at me, mewing sweetly, huddling playfully.

My fleeting impulse to catch the kittens and throw them into the street or over the fence into the vacant plot behind our house, to rid us of the cat and her brood, was soon overcome by a strong feeling of tenderness and compassion. I welcomed the newborns with a wide smile. In fact, I worried about their safety when I saw a flock of predator eagles circling the sky over me. The kittens had at once managed a catwalk into my heart.

I called Leela. She was ecstatic to see the pretty and playful kitten. Without asking any questions about them, without realizing that it was their mother who had caused us so much distress, she hurried back inside, came out with a saucer of milk and left it near them. We retreated for a while to let the mother return to her young ones and to lap up the milk.

An additional ritual started from that day on - feeding milk to the cat family. Over a period of time, the kittens ventured out of the drum onto the lawn and regaled us with their frolic. We even witnessed the cat-and-mouse games being taught to them by their mother. This truce graduated into a friendship as the little ones started bonding with us, slowly entering it into our living space.

And, by some unwritten understanding, the cat stopped eating the birds.

13
INSOMNIA

It was a cold December morning. A young man sought my consultation. Handsome, of medium height and fair complexion, he wore a green tweed jacket over a woollen pullover and gray corduroy trousers. He wore a tense, rather pathetic expression on his face.

"You are Abdul Rashid?" I addressed him after looking at his name on the appointment slip that he handed over to me.

He nodded and replied, "Yes doctor, my name is Abdul Rashid Magrey."

"So, what brings you here?" I asked.

"Doctor, I hope I have come to the right place; my family recommended your name. I have a terrible problem; I have lost my sleep." He spoke plainly.

"Well, well loss of sleep in a young man! There has to be a reason. Tell me more." I asked gently and reassuringly to gain his confidence.

"Nothing that I can think of," he replied without a pause.

"How old are you; where do you live; what do you do?" I started my routine questioning.

"I am twenty five years old and belong to Banihal. At present, I am pursuing a course at the Jammu University. I stay in a hostel." He was quick and to the point, answering the questions in the sequence they were asked.

"How long have you been here?"

"I am in my second semester, but I am worried I might fail this session if I continue to suffer from this problem."

"Any other problems?"

Yes. I cannot concentrate on my studies, my eyes keep smarting, my body feels tired and weak."

He seemed visibly distressed. I listened patiently, allowing him to continue. "I drink a lot of tea to stay alert during the day. My friends tell me I look haggard. They must be right, I feel worn out."

"How long has this been going on?" I asked.

"Nearly four months."

"What is the pattern of your sleep? Do you find difficulty falling asleep or staying asleep? Do you wake up too early?"

"I have trouble on all three counts. It is hard to fall asleep, harder to maintain sleep continuously for more than a couple of hours. I wake up early. That has been my habit even if I have little sleep. I do not feel rested in the mornings as I used to."

"Do you smoke or drink? Any drugs? Any thing else that you might want to tell me?"

"I have been a casual smoker but I have never touched alcohol or drugs in my life."

"Did you pass the previous semester?"

"Yes sir, I cleared all the subjects?"

"Do you have friends?"

"Quite a few." He heaved a long sigh.

"Good friends?"

He hesitated for a while and replied, "I think so."

"Your teachers, are they happy with you?"

"Yes, quite happy. But I may lose their goodwill if I do not perform well." He heaved another sigh.

"What about your family at Banihal? Is everything alright with them?"

"Yes, all is well. My parents speak with me everyday on the phone. I have two sisters and a brother who visit me occasionally. I go home every two or three months for a short break."

He seemed honest and frank. Nevertheless, I felt he was not coming out with the whole story. Was he shy of sharing his thoughts? Was his mind assailed by some nagging problem that interfered with his sleep?

"Well, you are a good student; you have a wonderful family and good friends to support you. Have you anything else on your mind?" I asked good-humouredly.

"No sir, not really," he said rather uncertainly.

"How do you fight the insomnia? Do you take any medication for it?"

"I get into my bed, switch off the light and try hard to sleep. I toss about in the bed but sleep evades me. Sometimes, I get so restless I leave my bed, go out and look at the sky."

"And count the stars." I laughed.

"Exactly. It is dark; every one is asleep, and the only things visible are the stars."

"Are there female students in your class?" I asked.

He was taken by surprise at this unexpected question. "Yes there are."

"Are you having an affair with any of them?" I thought that could be the most likely reason for a healthy young man to lose sleep. Falling in love makes one count the stars at night, strike friendship with the moon, and call the muse to compose poems. The twain—falling in love and going to sleep—do not go well together.

He looked embarrassed. "No sir, that is not the case."

"Don't be shy. You are the right age to fall in love and there is nothing to feel guilty or shy about it. Is that what is on your mind?"

"I feel it is not the time for me to fall in love or think of marriage. I have to get my degree and build my career first."

"You are right, but when it happens, it can catch you unawares, in spite of yourself." I was probing him gently.

"Sir, you speak from personal experience, it seems." He smiled for the first time and looked handsomer.

"The seed of love sprouts in each one of us sometime. If it is not love, what is it in your case, young man?'

"Religion." He exclaimed.

"Religion?" I thought I heard it wrong. Religion was the last thing that I would expect to be a cause of insomnia.

"Yes sir, religion has been giving me sleepless nights. It just does not get out of my head. I am obsessed with it. Though I have read many books on it, I do not seem to get anywhere. It has replaced my textbooks."

"How did you get into it?"

"When one sees and hears all the terrible things that happen in the name of religion, one wants to know why," he replied.

"But the study of religion should not rob you of sleep? Religion is supposed to lead one from darkness to light, bring peace to the mind and calm the nerves." I endeavoured to disabuse this young man of any wild thoughts about religion, even though he might have been echoing my own doubts about any good that any religion did to humanity.

"I feel religion all over me. There does not seem to be any room left for any other thought, for any creativity. I feel I am going insane with the bug of religion worming into my brain," he burst forth.

"Are you speaking of any particular religion?" I asked.

"I have been studying many religious texts and commentaries. The more I go into them the more confused I become. There is a clash between what religion teaches and what I feel is right."

"What is the confusion about? Where is the clash?"

He faltered a while and continued, "For example, I am not sure about Jihad, about conversions, about marriage laws, about holy wars, about fatwa, and about so many other things that my religion preaches."

This was the first time in my experience that a Muslim was expressing discord with his religion. It was not a disparagement, yet he was so worked up about it, that he had lost his peace of mind and was forced to seek medical attention. I did not feel competent to lecture him on religion, certainly not on Islam. Yet, here was a young man in need of help.

"Well, if you are not sure about some religious precepts, maybe you should put them aside for the time being and concentrate on your studies. No one is going to question you. You have a whole life ahead of you to study religion and find the essence that may be eluding you now."

"But there is persuasion." He said it so low he seemed to swallow his own words.

This was certainly intriguing. "Persuasion for what, from whom?" I asked.

He hesitated for a while as I looked intently at him. "From friends, peers and groups. We are being persuaded to be religious, to pray five times a day, to attend the mosque at least once a day, and without fail on Friday; to attend sermons, to study the *Koran* and to follow the Sharia. That is a lot of religion to practise when one's mind wants to be free to study what I came here for."

"It is your choice whether you want to do what others tell you or what you feel is necessary at this stage of your life."

"Unfortunately it is not so. We all live in a society and are supposed to follow its dictates. How can I extricate myself from my community? How can I be a rebel without suffering the consequences?"

"Then it is better to follow the crowd. Do what they all do as long as it does not harm you or others."

"But I feel what I am being led into is certainly not going to be of much help to humanity. You see, I have this thing you call conscience. How can I betray it? Yet, I am not able to get out of religion. It has taken a stranglehold on me. It has taken my sleep away. Can you do something, doctor, to put my brain back into the state it was when there was no religion in it?"

He was in obvious distress under a great load that was bearing down on him he wanted to shake it off and be free. I did not know how to help him. I closed my eyes for a while and sought Shiva's guidance–a practice that has been rewarding to me at such junctures. The lord smiled benevolently, "You pose as a preacher every time people of your faith come to you with their problems. Why do you develop cold feet this time? Just because he does not belong to the same religion as you? If you have no hesitation in questioning your religious dogma for what does not appeal to you in it, if you feel free to criticize your scriptures for perceived aberrations, if you find the courage to castigate the false purveyors of your religion, why are you in a fix now? He has come to seek your counsel. You have the license to think and act in the best interest of your patient, irrespective of his caste, creed or religion."

"I have the license to analyze and criticize my own religion, not other religions. You have given it to me. But in this case, my hands are tied." I replied.

"Your profession enjoins you to do everything within your competence to help your patient. You do not have to get enmeshed in the complex maze of religious dogma. But he can be guided to embrace the religion of free thought."

"That would be treated as connivance my lord, motivating a believer out of his faith into the freedom of spirit that may not agree with his religion."

"You are not going to do that, certainly not! Yet, he has a conscience he spoke about; did he not? Tap that. What is religion except the call of conscience? That is what you need to focus upon."

The dialogue ended but left me confused. I looked at Abdul Rashid again. He was waiting for me.

"Well, it may be a matter of interpretation. It often is the difference between the teaching and the practice of religion," I tried to comfort him.

"That is what I am worried about—the practice. I am not happy about the straight—jacketing of religion. I want it to be a source of freedom and joy. I want to be free like the child I was who knew no religion. I want to sleep like a baby again."

"My best advice to you is to follow the dictates of your conscience. As far as I am aware, that is a basic tenet of every religion," I said in all sincerity.

"I will try my best, sir. Meanwhile, what about my sleep? Can you prescribe some medicine, please?"

"Of course I will, to tide you over the present predicament," I reassured him.

I explained to him some fundamentals about sleep hygiene. I also provided some hints on the tradition of *yoga nidra*, which might help streamline his thoughts. Then I wrote out a prescription and handed it over to him.

"What are these pills for, doctor?" he asked as I explained the dosage.

"One is to stop your intrusive thoughts, the other to help you sleep, if other measures that I have described fail."

"How long do I need to take them?" he asked.

"Until you get better and start enjoying peaceful, restorative sleep. That might take a few weeks."

"I hope I do not go from one addiction to another doctor?"

"What do you mean?" I asked.

"From religion to drugs." He seemed quite insightful.

I laughed. "I do not think so. In any case, you need a follow up. I would suggest you report back in ten days."

He bowed and left.

"I have a hunch, he is not going to come back," Shiva winked at me.

"Why my lord?" I asked.

"Because you have not addressed the root cause of his problem. You have merely prescribed a sleeping pill and an antidepressant that may or may not work."

"Was there any other way I could have managed him?" I asked.

"You know better. Sometimes proscribing helps more than prescribing."

"I do not understand, my lord."

"You seem to give short shrift to the basics, my dear fellow. You have to empathize with the patient, feel his pain, suffer the turmoil he is going through, break the cobwebs of confusion that enmesh his mind. There is no short cut to sincerity in any profession, certainly not in yours."

"What did I leave undone, my lord?"

"You should have told him to forswear religion for now."

"That would have consequences," I replied.

"Irrespective of the consequences, you have a duty to your patient who reposes all trust in you to do the best for him. After all, you will be doing it in good faith."

Shiva was visibly upset. All I hoped now was to make up for my lapse the next time the patient reported to me. But, Shiva's hunch was right. Young Mr Magrey never returned. He was lost in the vast crowd of insomniacs who get treated for symptoms but not the cause.

14
THE SWAMI'S DREAM

Swami Chuni Lal was born in Handwara, 75 kilometers from Srinagar. He is believed to have been endowed with a spiritual streak since his childhood. Be it summer or winter, cloud or rain, snow or sleet, he would get up at three in the night, take a shower and visit the local temple. Often, the early morning visitors to the temple found him asleep, with his arms in an embrace around the large Shiva lingam. He had very little formal education. His parents managed to find him a clerical job in the Department of Education, and a wife with whom he sired three children. Aside from his secular responsibilities, he devoted time to religious rituals and practices that attracted a large number of followers.

The swami and his family migrated to Jammu during the exodus of Kashmiri Pandits in the nineties. His disciples followed him or was it the other way round, no one could say. In any case, their numbers grew when he landed in Jammu. When governments and gods fail, god-men take over. Ministers and mandarins are distant and unapproachable, gods imaginary and unreal, but god-men are always there—very real and so near. One is dazed by the aura from their vermilion and ash-smeared foreheads, mesmerized by their hypnotizing looks, enthused by their saffron robes, flowing beards and long hair. You touch their feet for real and they raise their hands, palms facing you in a gesture of blessing. Tormented souls readily feed on the spiritual viands that the swamis dish out.

Exile produced a unique ferment in the displaced populace and gave birth to numerous political organizations, cultural groups, social bodies and religious outfits. Many new swamis surfaced and built their ashrams and attracted crowds of followers. Swami Chuni Lal too received a share of the tidal wave of spiritual seekers. Over the years, he built a small house to which people flocked in large numbers. He would sit on the floor in a large room, on a raised platform of mattresses piled one upon another, while the aspirants tended to his needs, of which he had many, since he suffered from numerous handicaps and afflictions.

The swami was lame in the right leg. It is said that during his infancy he had a big boil on his buttock. A barber went overboard with his knife to incise the boil and drain the pus, in the process cutting the nerves to the leg. His foot dropped and the leg atrophied and never kept pace with the growth of his body, leaving him with a hideous limp. His mother decided to fight this impediment by overfeeding him. In the process, he gathered abnormal mass. Strangely, his lameness and corpulence seemed to add new dimensions to his spirituality in the minds of his followers.

Whenever the swami visited me concerning his ailments, his retinue of disciples helped place his large frame on a wheelchair and push it inside my consulting chamber. He would not even blink, or make any effort whatsoever, to ease the task of his acolytes. He wallowed in their ministrations, spoke little, and maintained an enigmatic smile while others did the talking for him. His over-solicitous wife, of robust build and much younger in years, invariably accompanied him. Always chatty, even euphoric at times, she took pride in tending to his needs. He was not just her husband and soul mate but a god. Her being was because of him, she claimed.

During his first appointment with me, I was overwhelmed by the number of disciples that accompanied him and crowded my room. Sensing my disapproval, they went out, leaving behind his wife and one person who rambled on with the details of his illness. It was a hard job for me to sift the grain from the chaff.

I examined the swami, wrote the prescription, and handed it over to the disciple, explaining the dosing instructions. Having asked numerous questions, many of them totally irrelevant, he fished a slip of paper out of his pocket, took a pen out from another and started ticking items one by one from the long list that he had prepared of dos and don'ts for the swami's diet. He had listed the names of almost all vegetables and fruits, fish and meat preparations, spices and chilies. There was a mark of diligence, sincerity, and solemnity in this young man, about forty years old, who seemed so taken by his mission of service to the decrepit swami. The wife was equally obsessed about the swami's diet and asked about the utility of bizarre concoctions that might provide strength to his weak legs.

After the consultation was over, and the other attendants waiting outside were called in to wheel the swami out, I motioned the young man to stay back.

"What is your name?" I asked him.

"Rajesh Bhat sir?"

"Where do you work?"

"I am a teacher in a high school."

"Are you related to the swami?"

"No sir, I am just a loyal servant," he said proudly.

"How did you become one?" I asked rather sarcastically.

"Through my good fortune," he replied with a sense of pride.

"So, he is your master? Pray what made him so? Does he give sermons; does he preach religion; does he perform miracles?"

He provided a simple explanation of his devotion to the swami. "I cannot explain it, sir. He does none of these things, but I feel happy when I am with him; I find solace and peace of mind. That is all. I love to do things for him."

"Yet, look at him, how helpless he is and how dumb. How can he inspire devotion with his handicap, his corpulence, his many ailments, and his crippled state? He has to depend on all of you and you have rendered him even more helpless, almost a parasite, by not letting him even move a finger."

I must have sounded quite harsh since he was visibly annoyed, but I was only trying to dig deeper into the psychology of surrender to god-men.

"That is a terrible insinuation, sir. We do it as labour of love. He is our king and we are his subjects. He does not need to even lift his finger so long as we are around. It is a privilege, an honour, to be of use to him," he replied with emphasis

"How else do you pay for this honour?" I continued to needle him.

But he was undeterred. "We look after his ashram and keep the hearth alight to cater to numerous visitors. We offer daily prayers and hold meditation sessions. We celebrate his birthday in a big way, singing devotional songs, serving meals to a large number of devotees who come to have his *darshan* and receive his blessings. It is a grand celebration of his sainthood," he said with a sense of satisfaction.

There was no point in arguing further or in disabusing him of his devotion. I regretted my remarks about the swami to a fervent disciple.

Swami Chuni Lal was sixty five. He suffered from long-standing diabetes and its numerous complications—hypertension and heart enlargement, renal insufficiency and anaemia. He was obese and water logged, his face puffy, his massive belly protruding and resting on his thighs, his legs swollen and blisters threatening to rupture. Yet, he seemed to have little, if any, insight into his problems, and was even less concerned about them. He accepted his numerous afflictions as a fact of life, as if he were ordained to suffer from them, and he did not seem in any sort of physical or mental anguish because of them, nor did he ever complain about anything. He left all the complaining and worrying to his loyal subjects who kept a close watch on his symptoms and reported any adverse changes in his biochemical parameters, and fretted and fumedx when a complication developed. He hardly spoke and never grumbled. His wife and disciples, who brought him to my clinic for check up once every three to four months, did all the complaining and questioning and answered all my queries.

It is not unusual for a person, who has remained out of touch with you for a long time, to turn up in your thoughts for no reason whatsoever. That he will also materialize in person soon after or the next day seems rather out of the ordinary. Yet, it did happen once when Swami Chuni Lal flashed through my mind unsolicited, and I wondered how he must be faring with his health. I even envied him for his dedicated bunch of followers and amused myself with the fleeting thought of donning the garb of a swami and having others to do everything for me rather than slogging as a doctor.

Next morning, the swami was wheeled into my chamber, accompanied by his wife and disciple Rajesh Bhat. He gave me his trademark vacuous smile. He was coarsely corpulent, with a close-cropped salt-pepper head. He sported a short shaggy growth on his unshaven round face, a large oval vermilion mark in the centre of his forehead, an off-white *janehu* round his neck. A dozen rings of different sizes, shapes and metals dug into the flesh of his stubby fingers, almost strangulating them. He wore a charm around his right biceps.

"Hello Swami Ji, what a surprise! I was thinking about you yesterday and here you appear in flesh and blood."

"When it is a call from the deep, how is it possible that we will not respond?" his wife answered for him. She was sharp and witty.

"Well, it may be a mere coincidence." I did not elaborate on the thoughts that I had of him the previous evening.

"On the contrary, you did call him," she replied rather animated.

"What do you mean?" I asked.

"Yes, sir, you did. Yesterday." She gave me a meaningful look.

I failed to grasp the meaning. "I do not remember having done so," I said, and turned to my nurse, "Did he have an appointment for today?"

"No sir, he did not have an appointment," the nurse replied

"We came on our own. We are here to show you the test results," the swami's spouse continued, and laid his case file on my table.

"Please look at the reports doctor." She looked at me as if posing an intelligent question and as if I knew the answer already.

"I must have seen him nearly three months ago. Did I order any tests at that time?"

"No, not when you saw him last. You ordered them yesterday," she said simply.

"Well, that is an interesting riddle," I responded, "yet I must confess, I do not understand what you mean."

"That is why I said you did call him. It was in a dream," she added candidly, as if it were normal for doctors to materialize in the dreams of their patients and order tests for them.

"Oh now I see! So, what transpired in the dream?" I asked the swami, waiting for him to speak.

He kept smiling at me and his wife carried on the conversation, encouraged that I was not dismissive of her explanation. "You appeared in his dream, doctor. You said you suspected a thyroid disorder and would like to order tests. Well that was a command for us. We called in the technician in the morning and asked him to take a blood sample to run a thyroid profile. We collected the report just a while back and decided to come here."

I looked askance at the swami, and he looked back at me with the expression of a child proud of having performed a feat.

His wife continued, "He saw you for real in his dream, like he sees you now. You looked at his eyes and said they were puffy. You declared that it was the thyroid that caused the puffiness as well as the swelling of his feet."

"I don't go visiting my patients in their dreams to tell them what I must when they see me in real life," I said laughing.

The disciple took his turn to speak. "But you possibly do it for someone like him. You are different from other doctors; you think about your patients in your leisure moments and communicate with them through thoughts and dreams."

I did not know how to respond to that compliment.

I looked at the swami's test results. Sure enough, they indicated hypo-function of the thyroid. I looked at him and realized that some of his signs that easily passed off as part of the spectrum of his renal dysfunction, from long-standing diabetes, could be partly attributed to thyroid malfunction—puffiness, slowness of speech, and his coarse features.

"I missed the thyroid dysfunction and he diagnosed it himself. I take no credit for it, or for his epiphany," I confessed in all humility.

"But it must have been on your mind, doctor. You must have thought about it. That is why you managed to appear in his dream. Moreover, it could not have happened unless you willed it. That explains why you invoked him in your thoughts yesterday, as you told us just now. And our swami transcribed your thought process into his dream, and we lost no time in carrying out the instructions you passed on to him. You see sir, it needs two people and two streams of thought to make it happen—the dreamer and the person dreamt of, the thinker and the person thought of."

I did not expect Rajesh Bhat, the disciple whose devotion I had derided several months earlier, to be so eloquent on abstruse subjects like dream analysis, telepathy, thought transference, clairvoyance, etc. This was parapsychology, a subject beyond my rational and scientific disposition.

Looking at me almost with the same reverence as his master,

Rajesh Bhat continued, "I had heard about your healing touch, now I see it for myself. You know how to do it—reach out to your patients through thought and deed, and even through dreams." He touched my feet in a mark of respect and awe as if I was revealed to him in a new light, through the twin paranormal phenomena.

It made me uncomfortable—his faith and his credulity. The swami had been the beneficiary of his faith and devotion thus far, now it was me as well. Just as I could not deny or dismiss the existence of seemingly unexplained phenomenon of matter and mind that one experiences in life, so also I had no reason to question the faith of a disciple. Perhaps the taciturn swami would speak and throw light on it someday. For now, I was obliged to add another drug to the long list of drugs that the swami was taking.

15
THE SOCIAL ACTIVIST

I was driving towards the Canal, along the two-mile Muthi road just where it begins, when I saw a hand rise up somewhat hesitantly for a lift. I slowed down, looked through the rear mirror and thought I recognized the face. I stopped. The person ran to catch up, opened the door and took his seat on my left, thanking me profusely.

Around forty, lean, short and bespectacled, he placed the polythene bag which he was carrying on his lap and started talking at once.

"Thank you for the lift, sir. It is very kind of you indeed. Who bothers these days? I took a chance. Perhaps you recognized a fellow social activist?"

I could not place him and continued to drive.

"I have been in it ever since we came to Jammu. It is in your blood and you remain an activist and strive for others even as you may yourself be in a mess. You know how it is, to feel for others, to do something for them, because you too are an activist. We admire your charitable spirit and your community service, sir."

"Thank you for the compliment," I replied.

"Where are you going, sir?" he asked.

"KK Resorts," I replied.

"You mean the *janj ghar*? Jammu is rife with *janj ghars* and banquet halls. Imagine the pomp and show, the exhibitionism, the utter waste that our fellow Pandits indulge in. And we call ourselves refugees! Jammu people laugh at us when they look at our extravagance while our fellow brethren live in wretched conditions in the refugee camps."

"Well yes, marriage halls have mushroomed and weddings are getting more and more elaborate," I agreed.

"But no one raises a voice against them."

"You said you are a social activist. Why don't you?"

"Who will listen to a small fry? Sir, you could educate the masses. You are well known. People take notice of what you say."

"I am not sure, really," I responded candidly. I did not want to carry on with this controversial subject. I had realized that no amount of argument, advice or admonition cuts any ice with our people. They do not care about the collective opinion but make their own decisions based on personal judgment.

"But the rich amongst us are setting a bad example," he persisted.

"Well, we are all to blame. Even the poor living in the camps do not lag behind in pompousness. They are wasteful in their own way. I think it is best if people are left to make their own decisions, good or bad." I cut the argument short and wanted to change the topic, since my companion was persisting with it.

"Do you have any idea about the road ahead? The last time I drove to KK Resorts, the highway had been dug up. They were laying the drainage pipes. I wonder if the work is finished," I inquired.

"No sir, the work is in progress and there are traffic jams. You can take a detour from a side street that will take you to Bhagwan Gopi Nath Ashram, if you know that place. Your destination is not far from there."

"I have heard about the Ashram but never been there," I replied.

"I visit that place quite often. That is where I meet people who help me in my mission, of reaching out to the needy. The Ashram does commendable work; it provides stipends to widows and medical aid to the sick. There are prayer sessions and lectures by enlightened men. They also arrange social events to provide our fellow refugees a chance for interaction, recreation and celebration of festivals." He was waxing eloquent on the activities of the Ashram, but I was scared of being held up on the way because of the pipe laying. I had an important engagement at three, after lunch at KK Resorts. It was already one thirty.

"How does one take the detour?" I asked.

"Drive down to the end of this road, cross the culvert on the Canal, turn left and drive another two hundred meters. You will find a large sign board of a public school on the right from where a side street takes off. That is the detour you have to take."

"Thank you, and where do I drop you?"

"Just near the culvert. Should I come along to guide you?"

"No, thank you. I think that won't be necessary, and you must be having your own work to do. I hope the bypass is not crowded."

"There are several turns on the way. I hope you will take the correct ones. You may have to inquire from the passers-by or from shopkeepers. Let me accompany you; you may lose the way. Your time is precious, I know," he again volunteered to be my guide.

I had been on this route once and had lost my way. I would not have minded someone leading me all the way but I hated to think that this person, who asked for a lift, should now be delayed on my account.

"I appreciate your thoughtfulness. But you have nearly reached your destination. It will be presumptuous of me to take you along and ask you to return on your own and walk all the way back. I will not like that," I said.

"It is no big deal for me. I have free time, and it will be an honour to be in your company." He seemed eager to come along.

"I am obliged," I said gratefully and continued to drive.

He went on, "It seems to me, sir, that you have not placed me yet. We have met a couple of times before."

I did not remember, and hated to tell him so. I merely asked, "Where?"

"I met you the first time in your clinic several years back. I had come with my wife who was sick. The second time was about six years back when you held a medical camp for the refugees at Mishriwalla. I was one of the camp inmates who were volunteering that day for your team. You examined a lot of patients, and dispensed medicines as well."

"It is always heartening to find young men coming forward for community service," I said.

"We do our bit, sir. The third time, you organized a vaccination camp against hepatitis and delivered a public lecture on jaundice at Mishriwalla. That was nearly three years back."

"So you live there, in Mishriwalla Camp?"

"Yes sir. My name is Bal Krishen."

"Nice to know you again, Bal Krishen. What is your vocation?"

"I engage myself with others who are in need. I go two places to seek help for them—doctors, hospitals, philanthropists, NGOs, and others. I do not accept any cash; I provide names and addresses to the donors and ask them to help the families directly. There are poor refugees who do not have enough to eat and can't fend for the education of their children. In fact, it is providential that I met you today. For quite sometime I have been thinking of contacting you regarding a poor family in our camp, who has no fees to pay for their son and daughter. The boy has been struck off from his school."

"That is not good. It is a shame that children can't go to school for want of fees. The least we can do is to help such families," I commiserated.

"The boy is in the twelfth grade, the girl in eighth. Her form teacher has warned her parents that she would also be stopped if the fees are not paid. The family is in deep trouble."

"That is cruel of the school authorities. Why don't the parents send them to a government school? I could put in a word with the headmaster and get them admitted. They will get free education. I could recommend them for a stipend."

"Sir, there is a peer pressure. Not many boys and girls from the refugee camp go to the government schools. There is a rush for private schools even as the fees go on escalating every year." He was stating the obvious, but that should have been all the more reason that the parents sent their children to government schools.

"There is a saying: beggars can't be choosers. I hate to repeat it for the members of our community. Yet, I would like to inform them that they can choose better options for their wards than go about begging for help to pay their school fees. I know some of the finest teachers teaching in government schools for refugees. The teachers are highly qualified exiles. Why don't you all send your wards to them to receive better education and have it for free? The government also provides a mid-day meal to the kids which the private schools don't."

"You are right sir, but in this case there is a problem. The boy I alluded to will have to reimburse the outstanding fees before getting a discharge certificate from his current school. Besides, he has another few months to complete his twelfth grade and it may be wrong to take him off his school at this stage."

"You are right," I agreed.

"Can you help this family, sir? You must know so many organizations that support poor families; you could put in a word. I have heard how you have been helping the needy without letting your left hand know how much the right gives for help," he said with intense feeling, looking at me through his tinted glasses, fiddling with his bag nervously.

"How many months' fee is in arrears for this boy?" I asked.

"Five months, sir."

"Well that can be managed. I do not need to ask any one. How much does it amount to?"

"Around four thousand," he replied at once. He had all the figures at the tip of his tongue.

I was astonished. "Do the schools charge such high fees? I spent just five thousand for my medical training that lasted five years and here you are telling me the school charges four thousand for four months. Which school is this?"

"Sir, it is not the school fees only. There are other expenses like report cards, printing charge for setting the papers, school uniforms, books etc. The schools find ways and means of fleecing poor students. Besides, the boy is also taking after-school tuitions from two teachers who have not been paid for two months."

That incensed me. How dare a family which cannot afford to pay fees for a private school also opt for a post-school tutorial?

"Pray, what is the purpose of going to a private school if it is not to save the after-school tuitions?" I asked.

"Unfortunately that is the trend in the refugee camps, sir. Just like the apple that takes colour from other apples, we are coloured by the place and people we live with."

"It is a pity that you should become slaves to an unhealthy trend rather than exercise discretion in your private lives," I said.

"But, we are looked down upon for sending children to a school for refugees and taunted for not being able to send them for evening tutorials."

"That is a pity. Does no one chastise you for going about with a begging bowl, openly or secretly, pursuing this outrageous course? Let us not be ashamed of being called refugees, nor guilty of accepting amenities, however meagre, that may be. But begging for special privileges is unacceptable." I could not hide my annoyance.

"I agree sir, but that is how it is," he said with total resignation.

"It must change; otherwise your suffering will never end. Coming back to the family in question, what is the father of the boy engaged in?"

"He is jobless, sir. The family of five gets a dole of five thousand. The husband and wife are at odds with each other. You see sir, poverty causes disputes and separations."

"Are they going to separate?"

"No sir; I mean they are always arguing and fighting with each other. The man does supplement the family income by doing odd jobs, but that does not amount to much."

"And the boy, is he hardworking? Do you think if he is helped, he will make it to a professional college?" I asked.

"I think so, sir," he replied.

"All right, I will take the responsibility of his school fees till he finishes twelfth grade. There are only three months left and I would not like him to change his school in the midst of his curriculum."

He was moved and caught hold of my arm in gratitude with such force, it took me off guard and the car swerved.

"Oh I am sorry, I got carried away by your generosity," he apologized for, what he called, his stupidity. I said it was all right.

While the conversation with Bal Krishen was going on, we negotiated our way through a maze of lanes and side streets and on to a narrow strip that flanked Bhagwan Gopi Nath Ashram. Here we turned left to the main road and another hundred yards ahead we were at KK Resorts.

"It is 2 pm," I said, looking at my watch. "You must be hungry and it will take you nearly forty minutes to walk back to Muthi. Why don't you come in and join the lunch with me?" I suggested.

"But, I am not invited," he asked surprised.

"It does not matter. The host will be pleased to have you. He is a good friend." I put him at ease, and he readily agreed.

We were warmly greeted by my host in the sprawling lawns of KK Resorts. He was genial to my companion, whom I introduced as a social activist. "You are welcome to join us; it is an honour," he addressed him, shaking hands with him.

It was a bright November afternoon of 2010. There were nearly two hundred guests inside the huge hall where the groom and the bride were seated in decorated chairs on a raised platform, receiving blessings and gifts from the guests who came up the steps of the platform in ones and twos. Music blared from the music system, and flashlights beamed from the cameras and video recorders. Having blessed the newly married couple and posed for a few photos with them, I rushed outside, Bal Krishen in tow, to escape the assault from the eerie mix of the music emanating from the DJ speakers placed in all corners of the hall, the chatter of people shouting themselves hoarse to make themselves heard, and the wild dance in which children were joined by adults.

Outside, on the lawns, an equal number of guests roamed about or sat in chairs around large tables. Others stood in two queues near the service tables—one for the vegetarian and the other for the non-vegetarian offerings—holding plates, taking their own time to pick the right pieces from the numerous dishes on the tables.

I met lots of people—friends, relatives, and patients – some of them seeking quick advice for their medical problems. Others spoke about Kashmiri Pandit politics, the many voices of our community leaders, their achievements and failures, and the shabby treatment of Pandits at the hands of the powers that be.

My companion joined freely in these discussions, enunciating his role in educating people in the refugee camps about their rights, which were being denied by the administration. He even made a scathing attack on Obama who had just concluded his visit to India, for not chastising Pakistan for their involvement in the separatist violence in Kashmir. When I explained that Obama had come begging for business that would lead to jobs in his country and not on a political mission, it made him laugh.

The guests moved from one stall to another, partaking of different dishes and delicacies. Finally, it was time for *gulab jamun*, ice cream and coffee and soon after, we took leave of our host and other friends.

As we sat in the car, Bal Krishen, by now heady with food and the discussion, declared, "It was great to meet so many people."

"And to partake of a hearty lunch," I quipped.

He smiled. "It was the will of Bhagwan Gopinath. On our way he came to our rescue and we drove without any bottlenecks and road blocks. I hope it will be smooth sailing on our return as well."

"The Bhagwan also provided a great meal," I put in, "warm sunshine, friends, food and gossip."

He laughed and observed, "Sir, it was a great experience to be in the company of some enlightened people. I made many friends who promised to help me in my mission."

"I am glad you did. In retrospect it was good you came along. I hope I did not delay you from attending to some urgent business."

"Not at all, sir. I was going to meet my sister at Muthi. I will phone her to apologize. I will see her next time."

We were back on the long straight road to Muthi where I had picked him up a couple of hours earlier. "Where do I drop you?" I asked.

"You may drive on. I will get down on the highway; then take a bus to Trikuta Nagar."

"That is far off," I remarked.

"Yes sir, I work part-time for a firm there."

"It is good you keep yourself engaged."

"In several tasks," he replied and picked up his polythene bag to fish out files and documents one by one, like so many exhibits. He started with his wife's prescription and again reminded me that I had seen her several years back and prescribed drugs which she still takes. Sure enough, my prescription was there and some more from other doctors.

"It costs me nearly five hundred to buy her medicines every month," he said and folded the prescriptions carefully and put them back in the bag. This was followed by some bills and receipts related to another person's cancer treatment, for whom he claimed, he was collecting money from various sources. "I collected money for a patient of heart disease, who died last month. I went back to a donor with the money that was unspent."

"Where do you get all this time for others when you need to work for yourself?" I asked.

"My wife too accuses me of neglect of family responsibilities. 'Why do you get involved in others' work when you have so much of your own that needs to get done?' she asks me. Since I have to go to various places for my work, it does not hurt if I can do a good turn to others on the way, I tell her. But she is annoyed with me, even angry, that I cannot maintain my family. She always reminds me how others have gone up the social ladder, even when I know what means some of them employ to get there."

"Your wife is right. We have to fend for ourselves and our families first; only then can we be of help to others—our neighbours, friends and relatives, our community and country in that order. That is how it works."

"I have been trying hard to earn honest money. I had to change many jobs, mostly working for others and getting a commission, or solve the most difficult cases. That will fetch you clients. There are so many divorcees walking the streets, looking for new partners. That is where your opportunity lies. The courts are full of divorce cases in our community."

"You are right sir. Why has this blight hit our community?"

"Because of the wide scatter in exile, because of the severe social upheaval and economic strains that we have been facing, because of the erosion in our cultural mores, because the world has changed, and so many other factors," I explained.

I did not realize that I was already near my home and had forgotten to drop him on the highway. I stopped the car outside my gate and asked him in.

"I will, next time, when you call me. Now I must be going, but not before I thank you for your kindness and for the advice."

"It is my pleasure. If I can be of help, please do not hesitate," I replied as we shook hands. Taking leave, he asked, "Sir, when should I call on you?"

"Regarding what?"

"Regarding the boy and his sister who are facing expulsion from school," he reminded me.

It had gone out of my mind. "Oh, well, I will let you know. Give me your phone number."

"Sorry, I don't own a phone; can I phone you from a booth?"

I gave him my number. "You phone me in the evening, I will let you know. I would like to meet the boy and his father."

He hesitated before he replied, "Yes sir, that can be arranged."

For nearly ten days there was no communication from Bal Krishen. I forgot about our chance meeting. Then the phone rang.

a salary that has never been enough. I have now decided to set up my own business."

"That sounds enterprising," I responded.

"You see sir, private enterprise needs initial capital. I have none. So I thought of one which requires little capital."

"Well?"

"I have just started a marriage bureau."

"That sounds interesting," I remarked.

"It takes no initial investment; you need a room, a few chairs, and a set of drapes to get going. I have none. And I do not know if it will succeed."

"The marriage market is hot," I said, "see how much our people are spending on marriages. They will be happy to pay you for brokering good alliances. In fact, with the wide dispersal of the community, marriage bureaus are in great demand. The community magazines have a large chunk of space reserved for matrimonial advertisements. Unfortunately, our priests who could help in matrimonial alliances, are a vanishing breed, and the old system of go-betweens has gone out of fashion. People are making use of the new media now. Internet, Face Book, Twitter, personal blogs etc. are the in thing. I am afraid there is no short cut to success in this line. You will need a computer to give your enterprise a good start."

"Once I get started, other things will follow with your blessings. I will know in about two months whether it will work. But I need to furnish the room first. Our people are quite squeamish. They must come to a nice looking office. The other day a 55-year-old asked me to get him a wife. Who will come forward, I wonder?" He laughed.

"I don't think that is something to laugh about. You have to

"This is Bal Krishen, sir. You had asked me to phone. When should I call on you?"

It was a Monday. I wanted some free time to interview the father and the son he had spoken about. "This Saturday, at five in the afternoon," I said.

"I will be there, at five." He hung up.

Saturday 5 pm, Bal Krishen rang the door bell to announce himself. I opened the door and found him alone. He stepped in and I led him into my living room.

He was carrying the same bag with him, wearing his tinted glasses, an outsized shirt, a red pullover, and a rather worn out light yellow woollen jacket on a pair of grey trousers.

"Take a seat and feel at ease," I said. "Why are you alone? Where are the boy and his father?"

He looked at me guiltily, took off his glasses, rubbed his eyes so hard I feared he might crush his eyeballs, and started cleaning his glasses with his dirty handkerchief that he pulled out from the upper left pocket of his jacket.

A long silence followed as I watched him curiously, waiting for his answer. Then he said, "Sorry, I could not bring the son but the father is here."

I was even more curious. "Why did you not get him inside? Is he waiting on the street?" I asked.

"He is sitting right in front of you sir," he said, jerking his head in a strange manner that seemed like a tick, his eyes without the glasses squinting while trying to focus unsuccessfully on me.

Was this a joke, I did not understand. Was he trivializing my endeavor to help a family in distress?

"I am sorry I do not understand this," I said in annoyance.

"Sir, the truth is that I am the father of the boy I spoke to you about. I made up the story as if it were somebody else when, in fact, it is me." He stopped and looked at the carpet, fiddling with the bag in his hands.

I was flabbergasted. I did not know whether to laugh or feel angry.

"Why this cock and bull story?" I asked angrily.

"Sir, it is easy to go and ask favours for others, but when you do it for yourself it is begging. I could not bring myself up to it. You can ascertain from the camp inmates of Mishriwalla about my bona fides, about the work I do for others. You see sir, being a social activist, I have been able to command some respect in the refugee settlement. I will be laughed at as worthless if I am found soliciting my own cause. I have always endeavored to supplement my income. I have not opened my palms to beg for my family. But it has not worked. Now I am stretched to the limit, and you were always in my mind as one of the persons I could ask for help. But I had no idea how I would approach you and unfold the agony of my heart. It was providence that arranged our meeting when you stopped your car for me on the Muthi road. There could have been Bhgwan Gopi Nath's hand in it. After all, my visits to the Ashram were not going in vain. I seized the opportunity when I saw you, and fabricated the story as if it were some one else I was trying to help. Now it is up to you to punish me for the audacity and falsehood, or forgive me. I swear, all I said is true to the last detail except that it pertains to none other than me and my family.

Why should I blame this person for being a social activist that he claimed he was, and for seeking favours for others while being too proud to solicit his own just cause? But, it was the subterfuge that he devised just within a few minutes of his having got in my car that stunned me.

"I do not know what to say," I replied, still trying to come to grips with the situation.

But he would not wait for me to let the subterfuge sink in. He opened his bag and placed a bunch of papers on the table beside me.

"Here are the documents you may want to see to convince yourself that I am not a fraud. They are the outstanding bills of my son, the school receipts, the fees paid and the balance to be paid for the last five months."

No doubt, the receipts and the bills bore proper dates, and the outstanding against his son, Rohit, was the same amount he had spelled out on our previous meeting. There was an outstanding of Rs1800 against his daughter, Diksha, who studied in the ninth grade. I had no reason to disbelieve Bal Krishen. All the papers looked genuine. In any case, he was in distress and in need of immediate help.

From the polythene bag he fished out the progress reports of his son issued by his school and handed them over to me. "I did not get my son here. I feared you might rebuke me for making up this story. I would die with shame if that happened in his presence," he said.

I looked at the documents. No doubt, his son had a good record. He had obtained more than sixty per cent in all the previous tests. I handed the reports back to him. He folded them carefully with trembling hands and placed them back in his bag. It was like a magic box that seemed to hold every device, everything that would rescue him from adversity and danger.

"I have no reason to reprimand you, but you must remember that social activism can come only after personal and family activism. You must try to reorganize your life; find a job to supplement your income."

"Sir, I have taken several private jobs to supplement my income, though I have had little success. The employers are selfish; they pay little but get work from you beyond the stipulated hours. They hold back even the paltry salary under one pretext or another. I must have changed nearly a dozen jobs in as many years. I can show you the papers." Saying so, he started fishing inside the bag again, when I stopped him.

"I don't have to see them; I believe you. What is the level of your education?" I asked.

"I failed twelfth grade and never got a chance to proceed. Militancy took over and we fled Kashmir and found ourselves in a tent in Jammu, living on dole. I started looking for jobs right away and changed many. I have worked as a runner for a pharmaceutical agency, a salesman with a cloth merchant, a marketing hand for a plywood dealer, a salesman at a stationery shop, etc. Presently, I am a commission agent for a company at Trikuta Nagar which sells modular kitchens, tiles, marbles, prefabricated windows and doors. Now, as I said, I have also started a marriage bureau. I have all the details in here," he said pointing again at his bag.

"What about your property back home in Kashmir? Do you still retain the title?"

"No sir, our house at Devsar, Kulgam, was looted and burnt down. The small land holding fetched a paltry sum with which my father married me to a girl from a poor family in the refugee camp. My in-laws too had fled from Kashmir and belonged to Vesu. My two children were born in the tent."

It was another tragedy unfolding. I did not feel it right to ask him to open his wounds again. I wrote a cheque favouring the school of his son for the outstanding amount. I wrote another cheque for his daughter, and handed them over to him.

He touched my feet in gratitude.

"Please do not embarrass me," I said as he put all the papers back in his bag.

"But you have been so generous. Nobody cares these days to ask if one needs help," he said with genuine feeling.

"You have been reaching out to others even as you have been in as bad or worse situation yourself. Your giving has been different. I gave a little of my money. That is not much of a giving," I said as I saw him off at my door.

16
RETURN OF THE NATIVES

Prithvi Nath Bhat claims he is seventy four, though he looks much younger. Of medium height and average build, and with a full head of graying hair, he sports a close-cropped moustache and metal-rimmed thick bifocals. Slightly stooped, more from habit than from age, he is a good conversationalist exuding confidence and optimism. He migrated from his village Gasi Rana in Kulgam to Jammu along with his family in 1989 in the first big wave of Kashmiri Pandit exodus. He left behind an all-Muslim village; his was the last Pandit family to move out from there.

He moved from place to place over several years to finally land at the Purkhoo Migrant Camp, specially constructed for refuges from Kashmir. Here he earned his claim to a room, twelve feet by ten, in Phase III of the camp. He was allotted Room 555 where he has been living for nearly a decade and half.

Prithvi Nath had withstood, stoically and bravely, the travails of eighteen long summers away from home, wondering each year whether he would survive another. It was like being reborn eighteen times. His heart was now yearning more than ever to go back to Kashmir. Go back at least once to his village, have one long look of the mountains, kiss the soft earth and drink deep of the sweet water of Veshav under the shade of a Chinar. After that it did not matter if he lived or died.

As the eighteenth winter of his exile came to a close and Jammu started heating up, Prithvi Nath grew restless. It would not be long before the sun would start raining fire from the skies, singe his skin and scorch his soul. Every year, he waited for the spring but every year it seemed to give him a slip, for winters merged almost imperceptibly into summers and summers into winters without much of an interlude, unlike back home where spring lasted a while and revived new hopes and desires, what with the thaw, the sounds, the smells and the colors that he missed so much. The longing to return home that revived every spring now became irresistible. No, he was not prepared to face another merciless summer in exile. Though militancy was on the wane and the situation in Kashmir had vastly improved, he might have to wait the remaining years of his life for complete normalcy. It was time to return home, he decided, for one last look, if not a permanent return.

There was nothing to go by except his judgment. That is how Kashmiri Pandits took decisions–through their own assessments of situations instead of following anyone. His seventy two year old spouse agreed to accompany him.

It was March 2008. Carrying two bags with bare essentials, Prithvi Nath and his wife boarded the Jammu-Srinagar bus, alighted at Anantnag and took another bus to Kulgam. Dusk had fallen when they arrived at their destination. River Veshav, unaware of their arrival, flowed quietly. Gasi Rana wore a different look from what they remembered. The road was paved, the alleys were wider than before, and many new houses had come up, with corrugated tin roofs instead of thatch, and brick walls instead of mud. They walked to their house from the village bus stop and found it in utter ruin. Other Pandit houses close by stood out like ghosts; they were either burnt down or in utter disrepair. There was no way any of these houses could be renovated to make them habitable again. He realized that he would need to rebuild his home if they ever thought of settling back in their ancestral village.

While the couple was staring misty-eyed at what remained of their orchard, a small crowd of teenagers gathered around them. It was the first time the boys found total strangers in the village. The couple looked out of the ordinary, out of place, and outlandishly dressed – a man with a boat like cap they had never seen before, a long tweed waistcoat with full sleeves, and pajamas with straight legs and not the shalwar that Muslims wear; and a woman in a short blouse and a baggy sari. The boys wondered if the couple had lost their way into the village, as they found them almost frozen in front of the abandoned houses, which, they had been told, belonged to the Pandits who had left the village en masse. Could they be the owners of one of them; could they be Pandits?

"We are no strangers here. We belong to this village and lived here all our life till bad times drove us away. Most of you were possibly not even born then. Your parents will know us if they see us." Prithvi Nath did not show the least bit of unease while addressing the bemused, inquisitive bunch.

Meanwhile, more village folk gathered and one of the elders, recognizing them, shouted, "What do I see? I cannot believe it! Is this our Prithvi Nath and his wife, Bhabi. Welcome back; welcome back to Gasi Rana."

"We are so delighted to meet you again, Jan Mohammad. How is Fatima? Your children must have grown up into young fellas by now. Where are Mohammad Shaban, Manzoor Ahmad, Mohammad Rajab, Abdul Majid…?" Prithvi Nath became breathless with excitement, rapidly reeling out the names of his acquaintances as if marking a roll call.

"Well, well, now that you are here, you will know everything by and by. Say, when did you arrive? You should have informed us in advance. Where have you been all these years? Did you not even miss your village? But first, won't you come in, wash and have some tea?"

Greatly pleased with the welcome and relieved that there were no uncomfortable questions, Prithvi Nath replied, "We arrived just a while back. Yes, we missed you all a lot. That is why we came here after these long years,"

"Now don't tell us you came just to look around or seek a buyer for your property. You must stay back, return here for good. Believe me, you have left a void here. We have often been talking about you and others who left. There is a feeling of incompleteness without *Battas* here." Jan Mohammad was still holding his hand.

"But there is nothing left for us to return to. We will have to start from scratch again. Our home is in shambles. Except for the walnut trees, there is not much left in our orchard. The apple trees have dried up, the poplars have been cut, and the almond trees are all but gone. We had sweated for the orchard, you know, but it has been laid to waste. It will take years to cultivate it again. By that time, even our ashes will have blown away," Prithvi Nath remonstrated.

"Come on, you don't have to worry about all that. *Inshallah,* everything will fall back in place once you decide to stay and give it a try. So many lives have been lost, so much destroyed in this *therik.* While the dead will not come back to life, all that has been razed can be rebuilt—homes, orchards, gardens. If there is life, there is hope," Jan Mohammad pacified him.

The crowd swelled in no time. There was commotion with people embracing the returning natives—men hugging Prithvi Nath, shaking hands and not letting go; women sobbing and shedding tears of reunion with his wife. There were spates of inquiries about their children and about other Pandits of the village—Ramjoo the grocer, Radhakrishen the school master, Nilakanth the postman, Shiben Krishen the pharmacist, and many others.

The village head, Khwaja Habibullah, joined the crowd soon after. The village Auqaf Committee unanimously agreed to take them in, make them comfortable and provide them accommodation to start their life in the village all over again. A vacant house was offered, with modest furnishings—two beds and mattresses, a few durries and mats. They were provided with utensils and cooking paraphernalia and stacked with provisions—rice, flour, potatoes, vegetables, spices, salt, oil and whatever it took to set up a functioning kitchen.

Thus Prithvi Nath and his wife began a new chapter of their lives in the village. Two girls from the neighborhood came several times a week to help with the chores.

People brought in fresh vegetables from their own gardens every day. Others dropped in to inquire if they needed anything from the local market or from the city.

It was the sowing season. Prithvi Nath decided to plant apple trees in his fallow land. Farm hands helped him plant and water the saplings and to set up a vegetable patch. He enjoyed tending to his land, chatting with people of his generation, recounting the horrendous tales of his life in exile, listening to the gory details of death and destruction that had overtaken the valley and the tragic stories of thousands of young boys, who had been lured into militancy and had lost their lives or were still missing. He was shocked to find young widows and orphans. He could not decide who had suffered more—the Pandits who were uprooted and forced into exodus from their homes or the young boys who were led into a self-destructive path of militancy or the general masses who were caught in the whole mess. It was Kashmiris who suffered; it was Kashmir that had been ravaged.

Spring transitioned to summer and summer to autumn, like Prithvi Nath had known a long time ago. He and his wife, almost forgot the blistering heat and the blinding dust of eighteen Jammu summers in the refugee camp. Though they missed their family, they spoke often on the phone. Their children were happy in the thought that they were safe and well looked after in their village. They had a bumper crop from their vegetable patch, the best ever that they remembered. It was shared with the villagers, the surplus dried for winter use. It would be an exclusive gift from their homeland for their children in Jammu.

Alas, the fall of 2008, saw the whole State of Jammu and Kashmir erupt once again, this time over the Shri Amarnath Yatra controversy—with the two provinces of Jammu and Kashmir at daggers drawn. The Muslims in the valley took to the streets, against the temporary allotment of land, for the pilgrimage to the holy cave of Shri Amarnath. The people of Jammu, including the displaced Kashmiri Pandits, also took to the streets against the revocation of the order of allotment by the government. Endless rallies and processions became routine in most major towns. All work came to standstill. Tempers ran high. Blockades stopped the movement of trucks carrying provisions to the valley. There were cries in the valley to cancel all trade arrangements with Jammu and seek an alternate trade route to Pakistan since the apple harvest was in danger of rotting. Many Hindu employees left Kashmir in the renewed wave of fear and distrust. Muslims of the valley were afraid to visit Jammu. Protest demonstrations turned violent and public property was destroyed. The Police were forced to fire on angry mobs to quell the violence. Lives were lost. There was communal and regional polarization— Hindus versus Muslims, Jammu versus Kashmir. The situation had turned full circle after an uneasy calm of several years, and was threatening to degenerate back to the chaos of the terrible nineties.

Prithvi Nath's children were deeply concerned about the safety of their parents in Kashmir. They begged them to return to Jammu, even blaming them for the preposterous decision to return to Kashmir. But Prithvi Nath seemed unconcerned. He was at peace with himself. He had lived his life. Having basked in the delicious ambience of his village after a gap of nearly two decades, it did not matter now, even if he were to lose his life. His ashes would mingle with the dust of his own hometown, where generations of his ancestors had lived and died. Nor would he fritter away the goodwill of his villagers. Prithvi Nath and his wife stayed put and never thought of leaving.

After the four month long communal fires were quelled, their son and daughter-in-law, along with two grandchildren, joined them and were warmly received by the villagers. It was yet another happy reunion. The youngsters were introduced to the village youth. There was good feeling all around. When time arrived for the visitors to return to Jammu, they felt sad. They loved Kashmir in her autumn glory.

"Come again and tell our other Pandit brethren that it feels incomplete and empty here without them," the village head said in parting.

December 2008

Prithvinath and his wife have come to Jammu to spend *Chille Kalan*, the coldest time of winter, with their family in room 555 of Purkhoo Camp. The Camp inmates, who had been greatly surprised at their decision to return to Kashmir, have come to hear their experiences of having resumed life in their village after eighteen years. They cannot believe that the couple had found the villagers so hospitable that they had decided to stay on and even resume farming. It seemed an isolated example because the experience of many other Kashmir Pandit refugees, who had paid a visit to their erstwhile homes in Kashmir to explore the possibility of returning, was different. Their neighbours had been happy to welcome them as visitors but not for a permanent return. On the contrary, they had offered to purchase their lands and deserted houses or whatever remained of them. The Purkhoo Camp inmates expressed their apprehensions to Prithvinath and his wife, that they had put in hard work to rebuild their orchard and farm only for the villagers. After all they were old, their children and grandchildren were in Jammu, and there was no possibility they would join them in Kashmir anytime in the near or distant future for a permanent resettlement. What was the big idea of their returning to Gasi Rana in Kulgam?

But this argument cuts no ice with the old couple. Come what may, they have decided to spend the rest of their lives in their village. It does not matter if their children join them or not. What matters is the thrill of resuming life from where it had come to a standstill after exodus, to enjoy the farming that they had done all their life, to live and die in their homeland. It does not matter if someone claims the farm after they are no more. What matters is the joy and spiritual fulfillment that seems possible for them only in Kashmir

Prithvinath and his wife will observe Shivratri, and give away *herath-kharach* to their children and grandchildren. This time, they will not have to purchase walnuts for the religious ceremony; they have brought walnuts from their own trees, first time in eighteen years. This time, Prithvinath's wife has filled an extra *vatuk pot* with walnuts. Two days after Shivratri, on the fifteenth day of the dark fortnight of *Phalgun*, the wet walnuts from the pots will be distributed to friends, relatives and neighbours. She will take the extra quota of walnuts along when she returns to Kashmir. The villagers of Gasi Rana, a couple of miles across river Veshav in Kulgam, are waiting for their share of the water soaked walnuts—a treasured gift from Pandits that will re-establish the much cherished tradition in the village after eighteen long years.

17
ALL ABOUT CHICHI

When we returned from a long stay overseas Chichi had come down with an intractable fungus infestation. She had sores all over her body-angry-red and weeping-wet-that itched so bad she got no time off from scratching till they bled and oozed and made us suffer with her. A bacterial infection supervened. Small and large pustules surfaced and the purulence gave rise to a fetid odor that made her ashamed of herself. She shied away from the family and no longer pleaded to be led inside the house, preferring to spend time in her pen, scratching her sores with her paws, licking them with her tongue and warding off flies with her withering white tail that once boasted of bushiness. She began to shrink, a skeleton showing under her shriveled hide. All that was left of her were her sad, sunken, somnolent eyes that would look at me beseechingly, begging for final release. I felt the sores almost on myself–a creeping, scratching sensation that followed me everywhere till I could take it no more. I petitioned the vet to put her down but he refused and there was no choice except to toss a handful of sleeping pills in her supper before leading her to my car and driving miles away to abandon her in a faraway place.

It has gnawed at my conscience ever since. Did I try hard enough to save her and restore her to health or did I give up the fight even before she did? The vet had tried his entire armoury in vain. I had augmented it with all my knowledge and experience of dermatology and mycology, but there had been no response.

I did not even wait to see her die, nor give her a proper burial!

I still get a feeling Chichi woke up from that heavy dose of pills on that moonlit night and is sniffing her way back home like the pet dog of an acquaintance who abandoned it across the Yamuna in Delhi after someone had gifted him a new pedigree. That faithful animal returned to his owner five weeks later, mauled and mutilated. How it had found its way back twenty miles through the maze of highways and byways, coursing through numerous neighbourhoods and crossing the Yamuna, is beyond the wildest of guesses. How must it have negotiated the mad traffic of the capital city and the abuse from street urchins? How many encounters with mongrels of different localities? How many refuse dumps and gutters foraged for victuals before finally finding home again, only to fall dead at the feet of its heartless master!

Chichi is dead for all I know, after that lethal dose. But, she has been sniffing her way back into my conscience since that day even as I convince myself that every dog, like every human, has a right to die, and every owner has the right to exercise the option to put to sleep his pet when its suffering is so evidently excruciating. That is exactly what I did; I executed a mercy killing. And yet, I cannot get away from a feeling of guilt and remorse.

When pain and suffering from terminal disease or from deep depression grow beyond endurance and when all hope is lost, one contemplates putting an end to one's life even with the knowledge that society will call it cowardice and that an attempt at suicide is culpable. Yet, how does a dog contemplate or attempt suicide? For that matter, how does a human being, if he is so debilitated that he is left with little strength to think or take action-go up the roof to jump down, or walk to the nearest railway line, river or pond and take the final plunge, or shop for a pinch of cyanide. You beg others to do it for you-euthanasia or compassionate homicide-before you are left alone to rot away, or condemned to a life of feeding tubes and central lines, oxygen masks and ventilators, catheters and monitors, napkins and diapers. You look into their eyes, as Chichi looked that day into mine.

No, I would not want any such measures for me that would only prolong my agony. But, can I speak for anyone else? Could I have spoken or acted for Chichi, my own pet, who I ditched in good faith?

But there could possibly be more to it than the compassionate end I chose for Chichi that may be weighing on my conscience and troubling my soul. For, Chichi was a darling, a playful black and white beauty who jumped and jigged with joy, and wagged her bushy tail on everyone. She was innocuous, hardly ever barking even at a stranger. She was so dumb, even toothless, and never bit anybody-except me, once!

There is a story behind that incident, though. A dog once strayed into our street and lay curled up outside my gate, peering through a narrow gap between the gate and the fence from where Chichi, tied to a leash near her pen, was partly visible to the vagrant. I tried to shoo the dog away. He had sensed her smell from miles and he would not budge from the place. I do not know where he spent the nights but I found him again next morning, and the next, his snout in the gap, his unblinking eyes on Chichi. She whined with pangs of desire while he would not budge from behind the gate for hours together, hungry and without water in that hot season—lovesick and love-bitten.

Chichi shrank as she refused food and drink and kept whining and tugging at the leash till she got a red circle around her neck that turned into a deep gash where the collar dug as she pulled. There was no way out. Either I had to let the stray in or let Chichi out. No, I was not prepared for the inevitable litter that would arrive. I had enough on my hands with just Chichi.

Chichi was gifted to us by a friend when we were forced to migrate to Jammu. His children were wasting time playing with her and losing out on their studies. We might need her, he suggested. She would ward off strangers and intruders in this alien land. We accepted her with gratitude. She took her rightful place in the family even as she failed to bark at strangers, not to speak of keeping them at bay. We liked her even more for it, as everyone praised her benign traits. In fact, she turned out to be less of a watch-dog and more of a playmate. In the process, as she grew up into pretty maidenhood, we forgot about her instincts, her desires and her needs.

There was a suggestion now, that we get her sterilized. But it was too late in the day. Meanwhile, what do we do about the dog outside the gate waiting for his love, wasting away with the flame of passion burning inside? Something had to be done for this transgression. I had to act before it was too late. I threw a small pebble at him, but he was not impressed. He looked at me with his pleading eyes and did not even make an attempt to move. I threw another; he just batted his eyelids. Did I imagine a tear drop in the corner of its eye? My neighbour, watching me, claimed that the pups in the neighbourhood had all been sired by Majnu, as he called him. That stiffened my resolve to send him away. The pups were such a nuisance that I shuddered at the thought of yet another brood from Majnu's romantic exploits. They barked at people who came to see me and created a ruckus in the neighbourhood. They followed me on my shopping, licked my legs, even jumped at the shopping bag to retrieve food. No, we could not afford a new addition to this pack of mongrels.

I flung another pebble at Majnu, but that had no effect. Perhaps he sensed that I was so half-hearted. No, he would not be allowed emotional blackmail. I looked at him severely and made threatening sounds. He got up gingerly, gave me a distraught look, and moved leisurely away to take position directly opposite my gate across the street near the electric pole, to inform me that it was no more my territory, and since he was no longer trespassing I had no right to get in the way.

I left him alone.

But Chichi became more and more forlorn. When I walked her for a stroll outside the house, she kept looking back and tugging at the leash to run into the embrace of Majnu who pined for her near the electric pole across the street. It was difficult to pull her away. One time, when she tugged with great force, the collar came loose and she dashed towards him. I caught her and started dragging her back inside the house. She snarled; I heaped a choice curse on her. She growled; I kicked her. That is when she found her canines for the first time, dug them into my flesh and tore a tiny bit off my calf. And that was her undoing. I leashed her again, pushed her inside the pen and came out with a stick to scare Majnu away.

That must sound a very cruel way to mete out justice, for it was Chichi that bit me but Majnu who received the punishment. Yet, I believed my neighbour that he was the cause of all the problems in the canine-land. This Casanova had despoiled many a virgin in the street and sired an ever-growing brood of mongrels. He had to be taught a lesson.

Majnu was not seen again in our neighbourhood. And Chichi never forgave me. She refused food for days together. We tried our best, or did we? Sometimes I wonder if that was the time when I started to neglect her, not giving her the regular baths, not walking her, not attending to that gash in the neck properly that took a long time to heal. And then I left for a long summer abroad, only to find her with the sores when I returned, that gradually became bigger and spread in spite of the last-ditch efforts and visits to the vet. And she grew more aloof, more sick, more depressed and ready to die. It is then that I noticed that look in her eyes. Was I the villain that came between the lovers? While I am haunted by the thought that Chichi may be tracking back home, my thoughts go to the stranger that came and sat behind my gate like a suppliant. His haunting lovelorn looks follow me wherever I go.

I have not looked a dog in the eyes since.

GLOSSARY

Anganwadi	Government sponsored scheme started by the Indian government in 1975 as part of the Integrated Child Development Services program to combat child hunger and malnutrition. Anganwadi means "courtyard shelter" in Hindi.
Ashtami	Eighth day of the lunar fortnight
Amavasya	Fifteenth day of the dark fornight (The moonless night).
Batta	Kashmiri Hindu male (Pandit). The expression Batta is sometimes used derogatively.
Breirkanis	Attics
Chaprasi	Peon/orderly
Chille Kalan	Six weeks of severe winter in Kashmir (January and February)
Churidar	Narrow, wrinkly trouser

Damaloo	A spicy hot potato recipe
Dargah	Shrine
Deedhaar	Audience
Dejhour	An ornament worn by married Pandit females
Devta	Deity
Doonga	Small version of a house boat
Hammam	Bath house
Havan	Fire ceremony
Herath-kharach	Cash gifts given away to youngsters on Shivratri
Inshallah	With God's grace/ god willing
Jantri	Almanac/Calendar
Jenab	Sir
Janehu	Sacred thread
Jihad	Crusade
Jinaze-gah	Funeral ground
Jo bole so nihal, sat saria akal	A Sikh spiritual slogan
Kafir	Non-believer, infidel
Kalima	The recitation of the words: lā ilaha illa Allahu, Muhammad ur-rasul Ullah as a testification of faith in Islam.
Karakuli	Fur from the fetus of a lamb
La ilaha illallah	There is none worthy of worship but Allah,
Mujahids/ Jihadis	Militants
Mallakhah	Community burial ground
Manzimyor	Marriage broker
Mohalla	Neighbourhood, borough
Naeirband	A multi-strand sacred cotton wrist band

Om nama Shivae	I bow to you, lord Shiva(Siva)
Pandit	Hindu of Kashmir
Panditji	Generally a respectful address for a Kashmiri Pandit used sometimes derogatively, depending on the tone of the address.
Phalgun	The month heralding spring
Phanda	Voodoo
Pheron	A loose garment worn like a robe
Pooranmashi	Full moon
Puja	Prayer
Qasaba	Women's headwear
Roti	A round loaf of bread
Sharia	Islamic law
Shikaras	Small decorated boats
Shivratri	A religious festival of Hindus which the Kashmiri Pandits celebrate with great fervour
Shraddha	Death ritual with oblations to fire
Sindoor	Vermilion/ orange-red coloured powder
Swargvas	To go to heaven
Tafreek	Pestilence
Takia	Bolster
Tamasha	Spectacle/ entertainment
Tathastu	So be it
Tehrik	Movement-here militancy in the guise of freedom movement
Tchog	A sheaf of hair on the crown like a short pony tail, worn by Hindus, especially swamis and spiritual men

Vanvun	Folk singing cherished by Kashmiris, Muslims and Hindus, alike
Vatuk	A symbolic pot filled with water and walnuts during Shivratri festival
Wazwan	Kashmiri feast with several mutton-based cuisine

www.ingramcontent.com/pod-product-compliance
Lightning Source LLC
Chambersburg PA
CBHW030046100426
42734CB00036B/211